MW00529846

Janet Kotler

LIFE
Goes On

BOSTON · 2020

Janet Kotler
Life Goes On

ISBN 978-1950319381

Book Layout by M·Graphics
Cover Design by Larisa Studinskaya © 2020

Published by M·Graphics | Boston, MA

✉ mgraphics.books@gmail.com
💻 mgraphics-publishing.com

Printed in the USA

In memory of my husband Vladimir Kotler

To my grandchildren
Jacob, Sara and Danny—with love

*My special thanks to my brother Aryeh (Leonid) Rigerman, my
friends Vladimir Frumkin, Ella Kagan,
and Anatoly Rozentsvaig — for their encouragement,
support, friendly critique and for helping me
to believe in myself.*

*My endless love and gratitude to my daughter
Marie Cochran for working with me, supporting me
and translating this memoir from Russian.*

INTRODUCTION

We've lived in America now for over 33 years, but I still remember the day we left Moscow as though it were yesterday.

Tuesday, June 9, 1987. We got up early, ate a quick bite, and began to double-check our packing one last time, stuffing the few last-minute items into our luggage: two suitcases and one carry-on per person, to fit our whole life into. Our close family friend, Masha, came to help clean up the kitchen and do one last walk through all the rooms; to tell her apart from our daughter, we called them Big Masha and Little Masha. We had arranged for our furniture and books to be taken by various people after we were gone.

A relative of my father's had offered to drive us to the airport in his own private car, still a rarity in Russia at that time. He took two of the suitcases down in the tiny elevator from the 14th floor of our high-rise apartment building, then came back up to get two more. Volodya took the last two, and the three of us and Big Masha ferried the rest of the bags down. In the elevator, Big Masha, in her usual reserved, non-demonstrative manner, made a gesture that touched me to the heart: she dug out a black tank top and handed it to me, to have something to wear while we get settled, since it will be hot over there, it's summer, after all... We said goodbye to her in the elevator; she had to go to work that day and couldn't go to the airport to see us off.

We got in the car and set off...

LIFE: PART ONE

I was born in Moscow six months before the end of World War II. I remember our "communal apartment," the Soviet regime's answer to housing shortage. Into a three-room apartment were crammed two families: the four of us (my mother and father, my older brother Leonid "Lyonya", and I) in two rooms, and in the third room our neighbors the Smirnovs: "Uncle" Vanya (Ivan), his wife "Aunt" Fenya, and their two daughters, Lyolya and Valya. By custom, Russian children called all friendly adults "Uncles" and "Aunts," even in the absence of actual family ties.

We lived in apartment No. 15 on the third floor of a long five-story building at No. 5, Vystavochny Lane, in a fairly ordinary, middle-class neighborhood of Moscow. All of its apartments were communal: two apartments per landing, two families per apartment. All along the length of the building ran a wide courtyard where children played in all kinds of weather and old, kerchief-clad women sat on benches, watching the children and gossiping.

The building had been built in the early 1930s to house families of foreign "specialists," those intrepid souls who had immigrated to Russia from other countries. Many were from America; like my parents (although I would not learn the whole story for several years yet), they had come to help build communism and to escape the hardships and privation of the Great Depression*. By the late '40s or early

---

* That story, which appeared in the 2015 family calendar put together by our cousin Elena Tenenbaum, can be found in Appendix.

'50s, when I was growing up, many of these foreign families still lived in the building, although some of the apartments had been reassigned to ordinary Russians.

Our apartment included a kitchen and separate bath and toilet rooms. I remember my mother and Fenya Smirnov negotiating the use of the single four-burner gas stove. There was a large window to the right of the stove, with a wide windowsill that served as a kitchen counter and food prep surface and had a large built-in cooler underneath that kept the vegetables cool even in the summer, and a single sink on the other side of the stove. However, each family ate their meals at a separate table, often at the same time.

The ladies often shared treats. Aunt Fenya baked delicious pirozhki for holidays and special occasions — pastries with cabbage, meat, potato or mushroom filling. My mother baked wonderful apple-cinnamon pies and cinnamon buns. Naturally, each set of kids loved their neighbors' food. One scene sticks in my memory: Aunt Fenya, flushed with the goodwill of these exchanges, says: "Esther Yakovlevna, I wish all Jews were as nice as you!" — and Mother turns away so Fenya won't see her face...

A radio speaker, a black Bakelite dish, was mounted in the kitchen, high above the sink. It belonged to the state, as did our apartment, and turned on and off by itself; we were not allowed to touch it. The same black speakers were mounted on light poles in major streets; they transmitted official newscasts — news from the battlefront during the

---

The tragic stories of that entire generation of foreign immigrants to the Soviet Union (few of whom ever made it back) are described in the excellent book *The Forsaken* by Tim Tsouliadis, published by Penguin Press in 2008.

war, announcements of arrests of "enemies of the people," etc. I don't remember when they were taken down.

What I do remember is the deep, solemn voice of Yuri Levitan, the iconic Soviet radio announcer, giving the Radio Moscow call sign. On the morning of March 6, 1953, he announced Stalin's death; his announcement was rebroadcast several times throughout the day. Stalin had been ill for a long time and had died the night before, but the news was not released until morning. For the next two years, March 5 would be a nationwide day of mourning, marked by memorial public meetings and somber classical music playing all day on the radio.

Public viewing on Stalin's body was scheduled at Column Hall of House of Unions, and later moved to the Mausoleum, red granite shrine in Red Square that already housed the embalmed body of Vladimir Lenin; Stalin's coffin would be placed next to Lenin's.

Another memory: Smirnov's girls are dressing to go to the viewing. I fuss and beg to go with them, but my mother is adamant; Fenya agrees with her, tries to soothe me, to talk me down. Later we learned that many people were trampled to death by hysterical mobs on the way to the Mausoleum. This was not reported on the radio; the adults tried to speak about it in hushed voices, out of our hearing, but we kids already knew it anyway from the women gossiping in the courtyard; I remember listening to them in horror and fascination. There was a lot of talk: the great majority of Soviet people believed that Stalin had cared about them and taken their welfare to heart; they called him "the Father of the country" and "Master" of the nations. Who would be our leader now, who would care for us now, what would become of us all...? And never mind all the horror stories that were leaking out; these could not have been his doing, they must have been the fault of everyone else around him.

Many (though not all) cried in grief and confusion; all were frightened. One didn't talk about it except in a whisper, with furtive glances over one's shoulder. It was all very scary and confusing.

It was especially scary for people like us. The infamous "Doctors' Plot,"* a trumped-up show trial of mostly Jewish doctors and medical professionals, was still fresh in people's memory. In January 1953, two months before Stalin's death, nine prominent doctors—seven of them Jews—were arrested on Stalin's orders and beaten and tortured in prison. After his death, they were all rehabilitated, released, reinstated at work and had all their honors and medals restored. For people like my parents—not merely Jews but Americans, who spoke Russian with an accent—all this was terrifying.

✳ ✳ ✳

I remember an escalation of anti-Semitism during that time, an almost palpable miasma of hatred toward Jews. It played into ages-old anti-Semitic attitudes deeply ingrained in the popular psyche. Many people really believed in the existence of doctors who had tried to poison Stalin. The radio and newspapers talked about "killer doctors", "murderers in white lab coats." Those who didn't believe this were afraid to say so out loud. I could not understand how doctors, whose job was to help people, could be mur-

---

* https://en.wikipedia.org/wiki/Doctors%27_plot

Esther Michael Rigerman
Moscow, 1950s

derers. My parents refused to talk about it.

One heard anti-Semitic slurs everywhere in public: at a bus stop, or in a food line (especially when tempers ran high because the food item in question was about to run out). One heard them walking down the street. I heard it once while walking to the store with my mother, my strikingly beautiful, dark-haired, bright-eyed, foreign-looking mother: a perfect stranger, a frumpy, untidy woman walking toward us hissed, totally out of the blue: "You Jewish bitch!"

There was always something to blame Jews for. My father used to joke that when the government ordered the arrest of all Jews and janitors, people would ask: "But the janitors, what did they do?" The punchline, of course, was that no one would find the arrest of Jews at all surprising...

Before the "Doctors' Plot", there was the official campaign against "cosmopolitanism"* — a code word for Jews in literary and artistic professions who were said to "grovel before the West" and "hate our Socialist Motherland" — a campaign that, like most such campaigns, began with

---

* https://en.wikipedia.org/wiki/Rootless_cosmopolitan

an infamous editorial in the official newspaper *Pravda* on January 28, 1949.

I remember that day. I remember my father, an issue of *Pravda* in his hands, calling my mother to come into the room that was farthest from the neighbors' room—the one I shared with my brother—and close the door. He reads an article in a low voice, so the neighbors won't hear. I can't understand much of it, but I remember the words "rootless cosmopolitans," repeated several times. Father and Mother are frightened; I have never seen such fear in their eyes. They whisper together. I ask what a "cosmopolitan" is, but they have no attention to spare for me; Father begins to say something but stops, makes a motion with his hand and says "later." I am scared. They forbid me to speak about this to anyone.

As foreigners, my parents had more reasons to fear than most people in the prevailing atmosphere of total suspicion. They froze when they heard steps on the stairs outside: that could mean that someone was about to be arrested. Their friends also looked scared when they came over to visit, keeping their voices low as they talked about these editorials and about those around them who had been arrested or might soon be arrested. Naturally, my parents made me leave the room, but I heard our neighbors talk the next day.

From that point on, my parents stopped speaking English with Lyonya and me and spoke it only to each other, in their own room, in a low voice.

If I were to paint that time, my picture would be all gray, even dark gray in places, like storm clouds.

WHO AM I?

S pring of 1949; I am four years old. It is a nice sunny day, and I am playing outside with several next door kids. A girl from apartment No. 18, Tanya Kochnova, starts picking on me because of my unusual name, Zhanna*. "You! Are! A! Jew!" Tanya throws it in my face — and laughs, and the others all laugh, too. This is an ultimate insult, offensive, intolerable. I must, I simply must return the insult. "And you... you're... an American!" I yell, before losing my composure, and running home in tears.

Sobbing, I told my father what happened, fully expecting him to hug and comfort me and agree with me that Tanya was a mean girl and had no right to call me names. What happened next, however, was unexpected. Father became very grave and said in a stern voice: "Sit down!" And started talking. He explained that I was both a Jew and an American, and these words were not mere insults but referred to real things. I was a Jew because Father's and Mother's ancestors had been Jews, descended from the ancient Jewish people. I was an American because my mother had been born in America. He told me that he had been born in a small *shtetl* (a Jewish village) named Kublichi in Belorussia, and when he was 15, he went to America to join his father, who had left for America much earlier. There he met my future mother, Esther. Henry and Esther fell in love and married as soon as Esther turned 21. They came to the So-

---

* As I would learn much later, I owe my name to an American actress Janet Gaynor, who was the first to win an Academy Award in 1929 for her film *7th Heaven*. She was Mother's favorite actress; I understood why when I saw her, here in America, in another film, *A Star Is Born*: Mother looked a lot like her.

viet Union in 1931, before I was born, even before Lyonya was born. They felt that the Soviet system was more just and equitable than the American system. Father was a true believer in socialism.

That was the first major shock of my life. It was hard to take in at first. What I did learn and understand was that one must never use random words as insults. After all, no one had ever, in my hearing, tried to insult someone by calling them a Russian or an Ukrainian. From then on, on several occasions, I was able to confound young bullies, when they called me a Jew, by calmly responding: "Why yes, I am. And your point is?" It was a pleasure to see their gaping faces. Later, when I was in 7th or 8th grade, I had a classmate named Lyda—a Russian girl from a working-class family; her mother was a cleaning lady and a single parent. I sometimes helped her prepare for tests. Once she

Esther Michael Rigerman
Moscow, c. 1935-1936

Esther Rigeman
with Father-in-Law

got very angry at someone: "That Jewish bitch!" "Lyda," I said, "she's not Jewish, she's Ukrainian. I'm the one who's Jewish." "But... you're... nice!" said Lyda. We had a little talk about it. I don't think I changed her mind in the slightest, but she never used ethnic slurs again in front of me.

I also learned that standing up to bullies made them falter and retreat. Especially if one answered in a calm, steady voice, looking them in the eye: they were usually the first to look away. This was a life lesson that would often help me later.

Nevertheless, like all Jews in the Soviet Union, we avoided these topics. We were all just "Soviet people."

Henry Rigerman
Moscow, 1935–1936

And though we might posture and strut among our Jewish friends, telling ourselves that Jews were smart, talented and hard-working, we could not help feeling like lepers, second-class citizens, marked men (and women). Virtually every new non-Jewish acquaintance who was not inclined to fling ethnic slurs felt the need to say things like "I like Jews," or "I admire Jews," which didn't help at all because it still had the effect of singling us out. They all knew who we were because most of us had distinctive last names, and most of us looked physically different from our Slavic peers. Most, but not all: people often told me that I, with my light hair and blue eyes, didn't look like a Jew. That's right, said my mother, it's just that all the Jews look like you.

That pivotal talk with my father made me understand some things I had never thought about before: why my parents spoke English at home, and why we had a gramophone, and a GE brand refrigerator, and a pretty mahogany dresser with carved accents and a fancy-looking mirror — things that no one else around us had: these were the things my parents had brought with them from America, reminders of their foreign past.

* * *

And yet Lyonya and I were happy in our home life; we loved our parents and our friends and found lots of reasons for joy.

My brother and me. *Moscow, 1946–1947*

I remember one winter; I must have been really young, not much more than a toddler, maybe three or four years old. Father is walking all along the length of our building, toward our entrance, pulling me behind him on a sled.

I am lying on my stomach, looking down at the compacted grayish-white snow that is gliding backwards down below. A tiny twig slides into view, and next to it, a small black hole in the snow. This piques my curiosity; I slide off the sled and begin investigating the little hole and poking the twig into it, warm and comfortable in my winter coat. Father walks on ahead, muttering something to himself; he doesn't turn around. Suddenly I hear both my parents' voices, Mother sounding angry, Father apologetic. Mother scoops me up, crying and laughing and scolding Father, all at the same time. Everyone laughed at him for a while afterwards, asking him how he could possibly not have noticed that the sled was suddenly lighter and easier to pull. But that day I cuddled up to him, wanting to reassure him, to tell him that I hadn't been scared but warm and comfortable, and that I loved him very much. He was very touched and pleased.

Since I was born in the winter, 10 days before the New Year, I would get sick right around December 20th (my birthday) or on New Year's Eve. It felt so unfair to be lying in bed, bored and fevered and with a sore throat, while everyone else around me partied and exchanged gifts.

I remember lying in bed in the room I shared with my brother, burning with fever and feeling very sick. My parents had already set up a tall, sweet-smelling fir tree but hadn't decorated it; we were going to do it after my birthday, but everything had been canceled because of my illness. I see myself lying there sniffling and feeling sorry for myself. Suddenly my mother sweeps into the room, wipes my tears off and speaks to me kindly. She wraps me in a blanket, carries me to the kitchen and sets me down on the wide window sill. Everyone laughs and claps their hands: all the Smirnovs, my father and my brother Lyonya. I am a bit confused but beginning to feel better. Uncle Vanya Smirnov, tall and broad-shouldered, comes up to me, looking very serious. He looks down at me with a big frown — then he rolls back his eyes, makes funny faces and strange noises, and then abruptly drops to the floor, spins around and comes to rest with his knees drawn up under his chin, wide-eyed, rubbing his head. Everyone laughs, including me. I feel supremely happy.

The New Year's Eve celebration was the biggest feast of the year. In the atheist Soviet Union, the secular New Year's Eve had supplanted Christmas and appropriated its trappings: decorated fir trees, a red-suited, white-bearded Grandpa Frost, gifts and parties. In the weeks preceding the celebration, people went looking for scarce groceries for their holiday cooking and baking.

I remember going shopping with Aunt Fenya in December 1946, i.e., shortly before the first New Year's Eve since the war ended. This is an unusually early memory; I must have been two years old. That winter there was no flour to be had in stores, but right before the New Year we learned that a truckload of flour had been delivered to our neighborhood grocery store and was available for purchase. The flour was rationed: two kilos per person — or into "one pair of hands," as the store clerks put it. My mother had already bought her two kilos; Aunt Fenya needed more than that because she was expecting guests from her native village, so Mother allowed me to go along as an extra "pair of hands."

For some reason, the flour was being sold in the basement, which we entered through the back door of the building. It was dark, dank and stuffy. The line was long and vibrated with suppressed anxiety, that constant worry

24

of the Soviet consumer: that supplies would run out and the last people in line would go home empty-handed. Fenya kept telling me to be quiet, lest we get kicked out of the line. But I was already quiet, engrossed in watching the people: their tense, morose faces, no one smiling, not even the few children that stood in line, as glum and silent as the adults. I remember the sales clerk's hands scooping the flour out of big drab-colored burlap bags and pouring it into customers' own containers; some customers brought cooking pots, others brought big glass jars. Afterwards, Fenya praised me for my good behavior, and I felt very proud and pleased.

(About those unsmiling faces in line. Years later, when we were already living in the U.S., I mentioned to my New York cousins, Gerri and Peter Gelber, that in our first few weeks in the country we all had noticed that our faces ached from smiling too much. Ordinary everyday life here involved much more smiling than we were used to, and our facial muscles were sore from exertion. "Why, didn't you ever smile in Moscow?" asked Gerri. No, I said, it just wasn't done. One didn't go around smiling at strangers: people didn't smile while passing each other on the street, and store clerks didn't smile at customers. Gerri and Peter found this hard to understand, but a few days later, Gerri called me on the phone, all excited: "Zhanna, I now know what you meant! I was watching the news on TV, they showed footage of Moscow streets, and I saw that everyone was walking around looking all sullen and morose!" This was especially ironic because Soviet media insisted that Americans were cold and indifferent people, their smiles a mere pretense, while Russians were all kindness and hospitality. Our first few days of interacting with ordinary

Americans — on the street, in the subway, in stores — disabused us of that notion.)

Sometimes the Smirnovs' relatives from their native village came to visit, and Smirnov's girls slept on pallets in our room. I loved those nights because Lyonya and I got to stay up later listening to the girls' stories, some funny, some scary.

Uncle Vanya Smirnov drove a truck for the Red Proletarian factory, and his wife, Aunt Fenya, was a server at the factory cafeteria. Every once in a while, when Father wanted to give Mother a break from cooking, he asked Fenya if it was okay, and we would all go there on a Sunday, and aunt Fenya would serve us lunch. My brother and I were expected to be on our best behavior during these outings.

MY NEW DRESS

For my fifth birthday, my mother decided to make me a new dress. This was at a time when there were no pretty clothes to be found in stores, and most people wore clothes remade from someone else's hand-me-downs. She bought a piece of beautiful fabric just for me, in soft green with a triple-check pattern in beige and a bit of pink.

We went to see Miss Fanny, who lived in our building and was known to all the neighbors as an excellent seamstress. Older than my mother, she was also from America and spoke Russian with a strong accent. We showed her the fabric and discussed the desired style; Miss Fanny even asked my opinion! Happy and excited, we returned a few days later for a fitting. The dress was beautiful, with a round collar and fabric-covered buttons, with a pleated

With my brother in my new dress. *December, 1949*

skirt, but... oh no... it had only one sleeve! How could I wear a dress with only one sleeve! I was about to dissolve in tears when Mother and Miss Fanny, chuckling, explained that that's what the fitting was for: to fit all the pieces together so they would look right when finished. Miss Fanny showed me the other sleeve and pinned it onto the dress. The dress (with both sleeves in place) was ready on time. I was so excited that that winter I didn't get sick at all, neither before my birthday nor before the New Year's.

* * *

We spent every summer at a *dacha*, a rented cottage in the countryside. I loved these trips. Mother, Lyonya and I — sometimes accompanied by our family friend, Aunt Maya Brin, with her son Misha — crammed into a big truck with a pile of bags, the women in the cab, the kids in the back. Mother always brought a lot of really good food, which we started begging for right away—Mother said that the sight of the first birch trees outside town triggered our appetite. These were happy times.

Sometimes we took a train to Anapa, a beach town on the Black Sea. The trip took two days, which was an adventure in itself. When the train stopped along the way, locals stood on the platform selling all kinds of treats: jam-filled pirozhki, homemade pickles, fresh berries, etc.

I remember our first summer in Anapa. We rented one house for all of us; Aunt Maya and Misha shared a room. Mother, Lyonya and I shared another one. Mother and Aunt Maya cooked together. The local grocery store was out of butter, so we bought a big aluminum jug of sour cream at the farmer's market and took turns shaking the jug for a very long time to make butter. I also did my part, although it proved much harder to do than it looked. Misha was too young to participate. The butter turned out well, with a slight tang to it. Both mamas were happy because butter was nutritious and provided essential vitamins for the children.

That was when I first saw the sea. It was as big as all the books said it was, stretching all the way to the horizon. It was exciting to think that there, beyond the horizon, was a foreign country, the exotic Turkey... But the sea wasn't blue at all, not like in the books: it was grayish-green. And the wonderful yellow sand, warm and soft, that felt so nice under my bare feet! I remember Mother and Aunt Maya spreading a big blanket, taking food out of bags, and all of us sitting on the blanket and eating breakfast. I have never had anything more delicious than those beach breakfasts, seasoned with a slightly salty breeze (and with occasional sand crunching in our teeth, but who cared!).

I remember running into the water, into the sea. At first, we merely splashed around in the shallows, in the clear water warmed through by the sun; further out it was deeper, and the water was colder. Eventually, I learned to swim, doggie-paddle style, and to float on my back, looking up into the blue sky with its white clouds...

After a morning on the beach we sometimes ate lunch at a seamen's cafeteria, which was on a small ship permanently docked there. We sat on deck and looked out to sea. My favorite dish was noodles with minced meat, known as "noodles Navy style." It sounded so romantic! Even now, decades later, I still like this dish and cook it myself, sometimes adding sautéed onions and tomatoes.

In the evenings, Mother and Aunt Maya went out to walk on the hill above the beach and took me along. They spoke English, and I asked the meaning of the words I couldn't understand, getting my first lessons in English grammar. Mother urged me to breathe in deep, breathe this clean, healthy sea air, so different from the air in Moscow, with all its smog and pollution.

* * *

I loved it when my parents' friends came over. There was a man called Zyama: he and Father grew up in the same *shtetl* and attended the same Hebrew school (*cheder*). I loved him for the mischievous glint in his eye and his sparkling wit. Periodically—especially when the newspapers came out with another broadside against "anti-Soviet conspiracies" or "enemies of the people"—he asked Father the same question, with his right hand extended, palm-up: "Why oh why did you come back here?!" His wife, Aunt Olya, was a senior nurse at the hospital where my father would pass away, years later. She was there with him in his last moments: he died practically in her arms.

There was also Father's distant relative and close friend, Uncle Borya, with his wife, Aunt Raya. He also grew up in the same *shtetl*. He worked as a communications engineer and traveled a lot on business, and one winter, he brought us fresh grapes from Samarkand in Central Asia as a New Year's gift. This was a magical event, because there was no fruit to be found in stores in Moscow. I remember standing at the balcony door, watching the snow outside and slowly savoring those delicious, juicy, translucent, yellow-green berries.

And then, of course, there was Aunt Maya Brin. Her mother, like my parents, had come from America. Maya helped Father in his work. Her son, Misha, was three years younger than me — in other words, Maya knew me before she knew her own son, a fact that I, for some reason, found exciting... My parents loved her dearly, as did Lyonya and I. Sometimes she brought a cake — a fluffy pound cake, sweet and slightly tangy and with a dusting of caster sugar on top. We called it "Maya's cake".

There was also Arthur Shkarovsky, a translator like Father, with his wife Faina. He was not from America but from England. He told us that he had been told by someone here in Russia that he spoke English with a strange accent. "Do I indeed?" he had answered. "Funny, that's how everyone speaks back home, in Oxford."

All these people, some of whom spoke with an accent similar to Mother's, sat around the table with us, told stories, talked about what was going on around us. They ate and joked and argued and praised Mother's cooking. Mother was an excellent cook and a gracious and cheerful hostess.

I enjoyed these visits—and the special food Mother served—so much that when some time had passed without guests, I would begin to needle her:

"Mom, time to invite people over!"

"Why?"

"So you can make your salad!" (Mother's signature potato salad)

Or:

"Mom, time to invite people over!"

"Why?"

"I want Aunt Maya's cake again!"

* * *

More of our family history came out in jokes and stories around the table. I learned that when Father was little, his father went to America to make some money, and at the age of 15, young Henry (Father) went to join him. I found out later that he added a year to his age in his travel documents in order to be allowed to travel alone.

Father liked to tell stories about his life in the *shtetl* and about going to Hebrew school with Zyama and Borya and all the mischief they got up to. He brought me my first collection of stories by the Yiddish writer Sholom Aleichem about *shtetl* life and about a boy named Motele. Later, he introduced me to the poetry of Lord Byron, in translation; for some reason, Father was quite entertained by the notion that a true blue-blooded English lord could be a great poet. Father also liked to ask Lyonya and me about school and always enjoyed listening to us talk.

Mother was born in the Bronx, in America. She grew up in a tailor's family and was the youngest of three sis-

Esther Michael
Brooklyn, NY. Circa 1929

ters; she also had a younger brother, Uncle Lou. She was 21 when she married Father and came with him to the Soviet Union. Mother had taken secretarial classes and could type extremely fast on her Singer typewriter, black with gold decorative swirls. I remember watching her and wondering if I would ever learn to type on it (I did) and if I would ever be as fast as Mother (I am not).

* * *

Sunday, August 31, 1952. Tomorrow is a big day. September 1st is the first day of school nationwide, and I am going to school for the first time, into first grade. I have my uniform: a brown dress with a required white lace collar. I can't wait to wear it tomorrow, with my festive white pinafore. And tonight, I proudly put it on, grab my gleaming yellow-brown leather book bag, and go to the kitchen to show myself off to the neighbors and receive their admiring smiles.

My bag is packed: a beginning reader textbook, a wooden pencil box, a graph notebook for math and another with lined pages for penmanship. I know how to read and count. Uncle Vanya makes me read the first page of the textbook over and over, making funny faces. He asks me to count to ten and rolls his eyes and sighs with exaggerated admiration. Everyone laughs.

In the morning, Mother walked me to the girls' school that would be my school for the next two years. We met the teacher, Yulia Vasilyevna, an obese woman with a short neck and a stern face. I was afraid of her from the first day on, until I transferred to another school. We did our writing in pencil for the first month, before transitioning to a pen. It was an ink pen with a removable metal nib on a wooden handle, which had to be dipped into purple ink in an inkwell. The starter nib approved for first graders was too flexible and very prone to dripping. Yulia Vasilyevna scolded me for these ink stains and gave me poor grades in penmanship. This torment went on until second grade, when we moved on to a more advanced, stiffer nib that didn't drip. Ballpoint pens were not allowed until 6th or 7th grade.

Doing Homework. *1958*

33

Also in my first or second grade, I remember when corn flakes first appeared in stores, in little blue and yellow boxes, priced cheaply at 7 kopecks. Later I learned that corn flakes were part of American food aid to the USSR. We kids bought them after school and ate them dry, sitting on the inside stairs of our building and passing the little boxes from hand to hand. How surprised I was when I saw boxes of corn flakes years later in the U.S.! Then we would go "to the Circle" to buy soda from a wheeled cart: 1 kopeck for a glass of plain seltzer, 3 kopecks for one flavored with red berry syrup. The glasses were actual glass (this was decades before the very notion of disposables) that could be rinsed before pouring by placing the glass upside down inside the machine and pressing down to release a squirt of water.

"The Circle" was a small plaza where several streets, including my own Vystavochny Lane, came together. Many of my classmates lived in these streets. In that circle was the terminus of an electric tram line, as well as several kiosks selling newspapers, cigarettes, and ice cream. The cigarette man, a tall, gruff man with a hoarse voice and smiling eyes, gave us leftover cigarette boxes, pretty green boxes with gold lettering — from Stalin's favorite brand, Herzegovina Flor, as everyone always reminded us. The boxes were left over because cigarettes were sold individually.

* * *

Mother often took me along to the grocery store, the same one where Aunt Fenya Smirnov and I had bought the flour for the New Year's of 1946. Our walk took us past a ramshackle green wooden house. There I met a nice girl my age by the name of Zhenya; she lived in the green house

34

with her parents, grandmother and older sister, all of them crammed into one big room separated by folding privacy screens. Zhenya and I became fast friends, went to school together, and remained close for years, until I left for America.

In second grade, I was assigned to the second shift: my classes started at 2:30 pm. I was supposed to eat lunch at home before school. I was almost never hungry, but my mother forbade me to leave the table until my plate was clean. I can see myself now, hunched over my plate in the kitchen, my mother typing in another room, when—oh joy!—my dear Zhenya walks in. Silently, I show her my plate, she says "Aha!", plops down on my chair, and polishes it off. She was usually home alone before school and too lazy to reheat the lunch her mother left her, but she was blessed with a much better appetite than me, so it was a win-win for all concerned. "Mom, I'm finished!" Mother comes into the kitchen; Zhenya, all innocence, stands by the window looking out; Mother excuses me from the table. I grab my school bag, and we run outside.

* * *

Lyonya and I picked up spoken English from our parents. By the age of four I could hold a conversation on everyday topics, e.g., at mealtimes; Father helped us construct sentences, and Mother helped us with pronunciation and intonation. She spoke in a beautiful voice and with a musical intonation. I knew the ABC song and "Thirty Days Has September", and "I scream, you scream, we all scream for ice cream", which became our shorthand for "time to go buy more ice cream." On Sunday mornings, Father came into our room and chanted: "Monkeys, monkeys, get up, get up, get up!" I knew what "monkeys" meant, but until 5th grade, when I had my first English class at school, I thought that "get up" was spelled with an "r." I told my teacher that this was correct because my father pronounced it this way, and he knew better. She kept me after class to tell me that I should do what she says in class and not try to show off, and asked to see my father. My father laughed when I came home and told him. He said that the teacher, Alla Lvovna, was quite right, and explained how the "t" came to sound like an "r" in certain words. After Father's meeting with Alla Lvovna, she began coming by occasionally to practice her English with my parents; she was a dedicated and enthusiastic teacher.

Alla Lvovna was also my homeroom teacher from 5th through 8th grade. She took us to museums, including the Moscow State Museum of Oriental Art, where I first saw Chinese jade carvings and tall calligraphy scrolls, and ivory figurines from India. She also took us to a candy factory where we saw how chocolate candy with fillings was made; we were allowed to eat all we wanted during the tour but not allowed to take any candy home. Of course, we probably couldn't have eaten more than two or three pieces each, but we were so afraid to let Alla Lvovna down that no one took a single piece. She had a marvelous sense of humor; she made our life interesting, and we adored her.

The same, unfortunately, was not true of our math teacher whom we all loathed, even those of us who were good at math. I wasn't, and she persecuted me every chance she got: yelled at me in class, never helped me catch up after I had been out sick. All my math teachers were like that, and by the time I got to trigonometry, it literally made my teeth hurt. I don't know how I managed to become reasonably proficient in math in spite of all of them.

With best friend Zhenya. *Moscow, 1958.*

In third grade, separate boys' and girls' schools were abolished, and I transferred closer to home, to an eight-year co-ed school newly built right in our courtyard. It was a large four-story building with big windows in hall-ways, which let in a lot of light. Several of my neighbor-hood friends were in my class, including my dear Zhenya. She stayed there until the end of 6th grade, when her family was allowed to move into a better home — two rooms in a three-room communal apartment, similar to our own, in the new suburb of Cheremushki, and Zhenya transferred to a neighborhood school. We remained friends and vis-ited each other regularly.

Soviet schooling, like all else, was above all authoritarian and conformist. In a 6th grade Russian language class, we were asked to write an essay describing a landscape paint-ing. The instructions said to make a plan first and to use it to describe the foreground, middle ground and back-ground, using adjectives and adverbs. I wrote my essay, exactly as instructed, without a single spelling or grammatical error — and in verse. My teacher, poor Rufina Vasilyevna, was scared half to death: she declined to grade my work, made me stay after school and rewrite it in prose, and gave me a "4" (a B grade). I was sad for myself but also embarrassed for her. I went home and told my father, and he understood and tried to comfort me. It is so nice to have an understanding family...

* * *

For me and my peers who grew up in the years after WWII, the war was a constant presence, a background against which our lives unfolded. Some of the neighbor kids from Building No. 5 had parents who had fought in the war and had returned, but the father of one boy, Sasha Vasilyev, had died in the war; one girl, Valya Zimina, lived with her grandmother and apparently had no parents at all, and would give vague, evasive answers if someone asked her about them. The boys played war all the time, as boys will, and often got into fights because no one wanted the part of a Nazi.

Adults talked about things that happened "before the war," or "during the war", or "while we were evacuated." We read books about the war, watched films where Nazis were always much dumber than our Soviet soldiers and officers. Russian actors playing Nazis, for some unfathomable reason, spoke Russian with a German accent (there were, of course, no actual German actors in Soviet cinema). We were too young to wonder how it was that the Nazis had won so many battles and had advanced almost to Moscow, if all the Germans were so dumb. Later, when we were older, we did begin to wonder, but these were

Henry, Esther
and Leonid Rigerman
Summer 1944

thoughts that could not be spoken aloud. But it was a fact that in the fall of 1941 the Germans had advanced too far, and Moscow residents were ordered to be evacuated to the designated alternative capital, Kuybyshev (now Samara), along with the government itself and all state agencies and enterprises. My parents and my brother Lyonya, who was still a baby, also spent the war years there.

* * *

March 6, 1953, first grade. The big portrait of Stalin hanging in our school foyer is framed in black and trimmed with pine branches wrapped in black and red ribbons. After the second period, upper-grade girls came rushing into my classroom and began to rip off everyone's white lace collars. I was appalled: my mother would scold me! After a confused interval, all the students were assembled in the foyer; all the teachers had red-rimmed eyes; older girls were openly weeping. The school principal announced that Comrade Stalin had passed away the night before at his *dacha* in Kuntsevo. The women started weeping during her speech. Words about "our beloved father" and "leader of the peoples" buzzed overhead while I stood fretting about my lace collar.

After the assembly we were dismissed. I walked down the street, looking at the tram tracks. When I came home, Fenya and the girls were home, with tears in their eyes. The radio in the kitchen played classical music in between solemn announcements in Yuri Levitan's voice. Mother took me to our room and told me to stay out of the kitchen. She never said a word about my lace collar.

* * *

Right after Stalin's death in 1953, people started coming home from labor camps. I remember playing outside with the others—it was already warm enough for spring clothes,—when we saw a tall, stooped man in an old and ragged brown leather coat walking along the length of our building. The women started whispering: "It's Pavlov, the one that got 15 years..." The man went into the building. He was the father of Lyuda Pavlova from apartment No. 16, across the landing from us. Later we learned that he had spent his most recent years doing hard labor in a Siberian logging camp. Two months later he died; from pneumonia, they said. Lyuda stayed inside; she stopped coming out to play and talking to us. The neighbor kids gossiped, mystified, wondering how someone with a quintessentially Russian name like Pavlov could have ended up in a labor camp. (And the janitors, what did they do?)

In 1956, the 20th Congress of the Communist Party of the USSR took place, the fateful conference where the new Soviet leader, Nikita Khrushchev, denounced Stalin's personality cult and his crimes and excesses. After this, many prisoners were rehabilitated (i.e., had their sentences reversed), and people began to return from labor camps in great numbers and talk about what was going on "in there." Some of us believed that, since these things were now openly discussed, life was going to get better for everyone. But others became even more frightened: since these things had gone on for so many years, what was to stop them from happening again, and even worse than before?

The stream of returning prisoners continued for years. They told of the horrors of labor camps; new and terrible facts kept surfacing. Years later, Russian writer Aleksandr Solzhenitsyn would describe all this in his novels *One Day in the Life of Ivan Denisovich* and *The Gulag Archipelago*. The former was printed in the literary magazine *Novy Mir* in 1962. The latter was never published in the Soviet Union. It was smuggled out and published in Paris in 1973; we heard it on Radio Liberty* at our *dacha* in the summer of 1974. The Soviet government jammed all foreign radio broadcasts;** Because of the location of the jamming stations, they could not be heard in Moscow except late at night, and even then only sporadically, but we were able to hear them at our *dacha*.

The 20th Congress marked the beginning of a relative relaxation of repressions and censorship, which would later be called "Khrushchev's Thaw."***

* * *

My father was a translator: he translated documents from Russian into English for various government orga-

---

* https://en.wikipedia.org/wiki/Radio_Free_Europe/Radio_Liberty

** https://en.wikipedia.org/wiki/Radio_in_the_Soviet_Union #Radio_jamming

*** https://en.wikipedia.org/wiki/Khrushchev_Thaw

Henry Rigerman. *Moscow, 1950s.*

nizations. He dictated to my mother, who typed on a type-writer, very fast. Every once in a while they would get into a loud argument over a word choice and over who knew English better.

Before that Father had worked for a meat and dairy processing plant as a book-keeper. A friend advised him to look for work where he could use his English, such as translating work, which also paid a lot better. Father quit his bookkeeping job and be-came a freelance translator. When I got older, he sometimes had me deliver finished translations to his clients, which included the State News Agency TASS* and the state radio broadcasting agen-cy**, among others.

His freelance status allowed him to work without being formally employed anywhere. This saved his life — and the rest of us as well. Soon after he quit the processing plant, many of his former colleagues were arrested in one of Sta-lin's purges and sent to the Gulag. The purges often seemed to be designed around some common principle, i.e., people of the same profession or people employed by the same or-ganization tended to be arrested together. But Father, who was no longer working there, slipped through the net.

---

* https://en.wikipedia.org/wiki/TASS
** https://en.wikipedia.org/wiki/Radio_in_the_Soviet_Union

* * *

When I was in 7th or 8th grade, our neighbors the Smirnovs were given a separate apartment and moved away to one of the outer suburbs of Moscow, newly built up to accommodate the growing city population. I went to visit them there a couple of times.

Their room in our apartment was given to another family. The man, named Vladimir but always referred to by the disrespectful diminutive of Volod'ka (I don't remember their last name), was a factory worker, a short man with a loud voice who was usually drunk and always angry. His wife, Maria, who went by the peasant nickname of Marusya, was pregnant. Volod'ka was building a crib for the baby and set up his project in the kitchen, where he was in everyone's way. One day, when my father asked him to move a little, to let him through to the sink, Volod'ka grabbed a chair and swung it at my father, spewing the foulest curses imaginable that prominently featured Jews. Hearing the commotion, my mother ran in and grabbed his arm before he could hit my father. Marusya dragged him off to their room, where he continued to curse for a long time.

As Marusya's due date approached, her mother came from their native village to stay a while and help her daughter. Now Volod'ka cursed and beat both of them, usually demanding money. The baby's first words were "Gimme money!" She never smiled. Naturally, we never shared meals with these neighbors.

As a result of all the trouble Volod'ka made, we were given our own separate apartment on the second floor of a new building that stood a few blocks away from our old home. The apartment was small and included two rooms, a small kitchen and a combined bath and toilet. It did, however, have a tiny balcony. Mother and I joked that Friedrich Engels (Karl Marx's fellow saint in the Soviet pantheon) was right when he said that people's needs grew faster than society's ability to meet them: if the government had consulted our needs, it would have given us a larger apartment, with a separate room for Father, who was already ailing.

* * *

In 1957, the 6th World Festival of Youth and Students took place in Moscow. It offered Soviet young people, isolated from the world by the Iron Curtain, an opportunity to meet their peers from other countries, to be exposed to different views on common human issues, to see other fashions in clothes. The dreaded capitalists and imperialists turned out to be regular guys and gals, who shared with their Soviet counterparts many of the same concerns and the same taste for fun and music.

This had a huge impact on Soviet youth, sparking a counterculture movement of *stilyagi*[*], who abandoned the baggy drabness of post-war apparel for new, in-your-face fashions. Boys wore short, tight trousers and brightly colored plaid jackets with enormous shoulder pads, colorful shirts and contrasting ties, and sported slicked-back hairstyles stiff with hairspray. Girls wore bright-colored fabrics and short, figure-flattering skirts, eye-catching jewelry and bright lipstick. At their parties, they abandoned their fathers' sedate tangos and waltzes for boogie-woogie, twist and rock-n-roll. For this, they were berated in newspaper editorials, which accused them of "groveling" before the West, of being ready to betray their Mother-

---

[*] https://en.wikipedia.org/wiki/Stilyagi

land for a pair of stylish trousers, of incipient criminality. They were publicly humiliated and reprimanded at student meetings at their universities and expelled from their Communist youth groups (the Komsomol) in an attempt to make them social outcasts.

The government and its captive press were not wrong to detect a social and political statement in this sartorial extravagance. In emulating America and the West, these young people were protesting the stifling, all-encompassing government control over all areas of life, from the arts and music and the life of the mind to fashion. They wanted to be free to express their individuality in their dress; to listen to music that wasn't all Soviet songs and marches about war-time victories and economic production; to speak and write naturally and not in the accepted stilted, pompously declarative style.

Eventually, the *stilyagi* passed into history, but regular fashions retained a greater degree of style, color and individuality. The extravagant *stilyagi* fashions of the 1950s morphed into everyday styles worn by later generations before passing out of fashion altogether in the manner of such things. Young people branched out into other, more direct ways of protesting Soviet propaganda.

* * *

1959. Fidel Castro comes to power in Cuba. Soviet media report his ascent as a victory of socialism. They call Cuba "Freedom Island" and "Fire Island." TV footage of Cuban events appears often in the news. TV channels — all three of them — show a popular Soviet singer belting out a song in praise of Fidel and the new Cuban regime. Fidel Castro is often photographed with a beautiful young woman by his side holding a machine gun. I remember her because her name, like mine, was Janet. A few months later she disappeared from the TV images; when I asked why, Father said she had been killed by order of Fidel, who felt she had betrayed the revolution. This wasn't on the radio.

* * *

At the end of 8th grade, in 1960, the school administration gave us a graduation party, with a talent show and dancing well into the night, in order to keep us away from a procession that was being held that night by the Church of the Deposition of the Robe in our neighborhood.

When they came to power in October 1917, the Bolsheviks instituted state atheism. They declared that there was no God, that he had been invented by the priests, and misquoted Karl Marx to say that religion was the opiate of the masses*. Marx had actually said that religion was a comfort, a humanizing influence, but they turned it into a mind-altering drug.

Naturally, some of us snuck out of the party to go see the procession. We couldn't see much behind the tall wrought-iron fence, but when we climbed up on it we could see the priest in his long robes carrying a big cross on a long stick. I couldn't stay to see more because it was already late and I had to go home.

And yet we all knew someone who believed in God and went to church. Although many churches had been closed and desecrated, turned into warehouses or offices, the country had been so profoundly devout prior to the October

---

* https://en.wikipedia.org/wiki/Opium_of_the_people

Revolution that the Bolsheviks hadn't dared to outlaw religion completely, and the Orthodox Church survived in a state of uneasy truce—some would say, unconscionable collaboration—with the state. Our neighbors the Smirnovs went to church on Sundays, and for Easter, Fenya made the traditional painted eggs and baked special cakes, which she took to church to have them sprinkled with holy water and prayed over. She talked about God who loved everyone.

2 yrs old Henry Rigerman with his mother. *Kublichi. Belorussia.*

My parents didn't believe in God. My father's mother was a deeply observant Jew from a very religious family. They kept kosher and celebrated Jewish holidays and lived in a *shtetl* where all children went to Hebrew school. During his time in America, my father came to believe in socialism and communism— a religion in its own right, which had no room for God. My mother's American Jewish family was not very observant either.

* * *

After graduation, I went to a new school to complete my 10-year secondary education. The new school was on Leninsky Prospect, a 20-minute trolleybus ride away.

47

The kids in my class were fairly nice, and although I wasn't interested in any of the boys I made a few friends among the girls. Two of my new friends talked me into skipping school one day to go see the new department store "Synthetica," the first of its kind in Moscow, that had just opened in Leninsky Prospect, three blocks away from our school. I had never skipped school before, but the temptation was too strong. We met at the home of one of the girls and waited: the store opened an hour later than classes started at school. The reality fell short of expectation. We saw snow-white melamine dinnerware that was different from the ordinary ceramic dishes we knew; we saw pretty, brightly colored nylon scarves, dainty lingerie made from silky synthetic materials, and other miscellanea, like sewing supplies, etc.; the store was more spacious and better-lit than ordinary stores, but it was still just a store. I never skipped school again, neither in high school nor in college.

* * *

1961, 9th grade. One day Mother and I were standing in the hallway when we heard the radio in the kitchen broadcasting Khrushchev's speech to the 22nd Congress of the Communist Party. "The current generation of Soviet people will live under communism!" said Khrushchev, sounding grave and solemn. It seemed laughable. At school, they taught us that socialism was about rewards being proportional to contribution: "From each according to his abilities, to each according to his labor." Communism was "From each according to his abilities, to each according to his needs." Here was Khrushchev, saying for the record that socialism had been perfected to the point that the country was ready to transition to communism and would actually do so — by 1980! Somehow people's nature would miraculously change in less than twenty years, so that people like our neighbor Volod'ka would quit drinking and brawling and would begin to work hard. And people would stop engaging in embezzlement and stealing, and stores would come to be filled with abundant food and consumer goods... It was so clearly a fantasy.

We all kept a straight face in class and didn't dare challenge our teachers when they told us this, but at home we joked about it. Such was our double-sided life: we didn't ask awkward questions outside the home and tried to conform, to behave like everyone else, but at home we could joke and even argue. Father was still a Communist at heart (he believed that the horrors and abuses were the fault of Stalin's underlings, that Stalin himself never knew about them), while Mother was more skeptical. Even at home, though, these conversations were conducted in near-whispers and behind closed doors, so that the neighbors would not overhear.

* * *

That year I turned 16, the official voting age. I was issued my internal passport — my official Soviet ID — and proudly went to vote with my parents. There was a big fuss made on the radio and on TV about the election. Posters on walls and billboards everywhere proclaimed: "Turn out the vote for the Council of People's Deputies!" "Vote for candidates from the unbreakable electoral bloc of Communists and the unaffiliated!" "Everyone must vote for candidates to the Supreme Council of the USSR. The People and the Party are one!" On the day of the election, solemn classical music blared from the loud-speakers. TV channels showed re-runs of films about Socialist workers' accomplishments. The films starred the glamorous Soviet movie star Lyubov Orlova, striding across factory floors or through fields of wheat under a blue, sunlit sky with fluffy white clouds in it, conveying a sense of purpose and exhilaration, to the sound of unbearably positive songs in major key.

Zhanna Rigerman. *Moscow, 16 years old.*

At the polling place stood large, pillar-shaped ballot boxes. There were also cubicles with fabric-covered walls, with the same kind of ballot boxes inside, where one could cast one's ballot in privacy. The ballots were pre-printed with the names of candidates, only one for each position, so this was really more of an exercise in conformity than an election in any substantive sense: theoretically, the single-candidate system allowed for a "no" vote, but I can't imagine that anyone ever did that. I wanted to cast my ballot in one of the cubicles but Mother worried that this might attract attention, which was to be avoided at all costs. Nevertheless, I ducked inside a cubicle to see, leaving the curtains open, but immediately came out again and demonstratively cast my ballot out on the open floor, to satisfy any onlookers.

The results of the election were broadcast on the evening news. All the candidates had been elected by a landslide (just short of 100%, to preserve the decencies). All in all, I found it a disappointing experience. But participation was mandatory; community organizers went door to door all day long, checking names off on their lists, badgering laggards to go out and vote.

* * *

One recurring feature of each election was food. The centrally planned economy kept the country in a state of perennial shortage, or, in Soviet-speak, "deficit." Periodically, there would be a "deficit" of chicken, or cheese, or flour, producing those long, snaking, quarrelsome food lines that have become emblematic of the Soviet regime. However, "deficit" goods miraculously appeared at special and important events, like the elections. At the polling place, flowers stood in vases on long tables covered with white cloth, and long-forgotten luxuries—like boxes of chocolates, jars of red and black caviar, special sliced sausage, etc.—lay on platters. They weren't just given out for free though, but sold by young helpers stationed behind the tables.

There were, in that supposedly classless society, groups of people who were "more equal than others" and as a result, less affected by the "deficit." Communist Party officials, government officials, and other select groups had access to special stores where they could buy "deficit" foods in season or out of season. There were also special cafeterias—e.g. at the Kremlin or at the Central Party Committee building—where these servants of the people could enjoy a better diet than the plebes and even take a box of food home. These special stores were also ranked according to the status of the clientele; the best stores served the top levels of the Party and government.

These degrees of privilege created envy and fear, both very effective means of social control. People who had a bit of privilege to preserve were less given to social or political criticism. Older people—who had gone through the purges of the 1930s (especially 1937), and then the war, and then the purges of the 1950s—also tended to avoid sensitive subjects. Both of these dynamics came together in my husband Volodya's father, who, as a war veteran and retired army officer, was entitled to some privilege, such as holiday packages of "deficit" foods: better-quality meat, fish, ham, special sausage, etc. Though a decent and nonviolent man, he was cautious and reserved; the kinds of conversations that went on in my home were unthinkable around him.

* * *

We were fortunate in our 9th grade literature teacher, Eduard Orestovich Konokotin. He assigned us reading that went beyond the official curriculum and encouraged open discussion in class, challenging us to think for ourselves. One of the debates he set up was "Let's Argue About Taste"; the prompt referred to the Russian version of the adage "there is no accounting for taste" and suggested that it was a good thing if different people felt differently about books, works of art, etc.; moreover, exposure to other views might expand one's own horizons. All of that was highly unusual and even unsafe in those times, which discouraged individuality and demanded conformity in all things, including literary and artistic tastes.

Zhanna Rigerman
Discussion about Taste.
9th grade.

(He went so far as to invite his most enthusiastic students home, telling us things that were definitely not safe to talk about at school. For example, he told us about his father, Polish Communist Orest Nikolayevich Konokotin, who had perished in the Gulag on a particularly absurd fabricated charge: he was accused of being someone else who had murdered and impersonated the Polish Communist Orest Nikolayevich Konokotin.)

In this, he was building on a specifically Russian tradition that predated the Revolution and elevated literature and especially poetry to a very important and respected role in society, at least in the cities. My family and friends, and everyone I knew, were readers; books were a frequent topic of conversation; poetry so permeated the fabric of our thought that we often quoted verses and images in conversation and argument.

When Bolsheviks came to power, they preserved the hallowed role of the written word, albeit under strict censorship. They censored both content and style. Most officially approved literature was upbeat and extolled the lives of workers and peasants under the wise leadership of the beloved Communist Party.

The 1960s brought a new wave of young poets and writers who wrote differently and about different things. Under Khrushchev's Thaw, some—but not all—of their work was published in literary magazines, including the popular *Yunost* (Youth), which my fellow students and I read voraciously, debating the relative merit of the poet Robert Rozhdestvensky versus that of Andrey Voznesensky. The poets also held unofficial public readings of their unpublished poetry in Mayakovsky Square in Moscow, named after the poet Vladimir Mayakovsky. These meetings, held around the poet's statue, always attracted great crowds of people, so we tried to come early to find a good spot from which to hear.

One of these new poets was Yevgeny Yevtushenko. We lived and breathed his poetry, quoted it endlessly to one another. He evoked controversy: some accused him of having "sold out" to the regime, others of being a show-off, but all agreed that he was a great poet. It was Yevtushenko who said in one of his poems: "In Russia, a poet is more than just a poet." He was right: in the absence of an outlet for free political and social discourse and debate, poetry took on a quasi-sacral role. The poet became the conscience of the nation, its oracle, teacher and judge. He published a sensational poem Babiy Yar, about the Nazi massacre of Jews at the eponymous site in the Ukraine, protesting the Soviet regime's refusal to acknowledge the massacre as a crime specifically against Jews. This was the time when the Holocaust as a uniquely Jewish tragedy (separate from the general suffering of the Russian people in World War II) was still taboo. One day I went to his home with two other 9th grade girls to invite him to come and give a reading at our school. We were greeted by his wife, Bella Akhmadulina, another great poet of the Sixties, who opened the door with a mop in her hand just like any other housewife. She said he couldn't come to our show because he was away in Cuba.

The poets of the Sixties were trail-blazers in that—instead of the standard platitudes about the Soviet regime, socialism and communism, the Party and all our dear leaders—they dared express their true, heart-felt thoughts and feelings and those of actual, real people, unofficial and unfiltered. Some of them had gone through labor camps, some had fought in the war or had parents who had done so, and this could not help but color their words. They didn't call for regime change, they made no threats. They simply wrote the truth: the truth about human feelings and relationships, the truth about the war and our daily life. But that truth was subversive by its very nature because it was the truth of people as individuals rather than as part of the collective. So revolutionary it was that some think that it was they, the sixtiers, who cracked the foundation of the Soviet regime and eventually brought about the fall of the Soviet Union.

This emphasis on the individual flew in the face of the foundational Soviet principle, often explicitly stated in Stalin's times, that all of us ordinary people were but cogs in the great machine engaged in building a new society. And cogs had no right to independent thought or individual opinion. The cogs were also interchangeable and easily replaceable. By the 1960s, this theme had become less prominent in public discourse, but the principle remained, so that the same Nikita Khrushchev who had originally allowed the flowering of the new literature, now attended a conference of young writers and berated them for their ideological and artistic sins. (He did the same at an art show featuring works by trailblazing young artists, where he reportedly went as far as to stomp his feet in his wrath, accusing them—especially the Abstractionists—of painting "like that" because they didn't have enough

55

skill even to "paint a cow." But what if they did, and instead painted "like that" for valid artistic reasons? There was much debate about it going on all around me.) However, times had indeed changed, and most of the writers and artists were not arrested, although their careers suffered.

Besides *Yunost*, there were many other literary magazines publishing serialized works by Soviet and foreign writers. Foreign literature from a wide range of countries began to be more accessible in those years, in translations by the many brilliant Russian translators. In this way, we were exposed to the work of most major Western writers.

✻ ✻ ✻

Music was another major influence in my life. There was a girl in my building named Inna, who lived with her mother and attended some other school. She had her own record player and a lot of vinyl recordings of classical music. We became friends; it was at her place that I first heard Rachmaninoff's second piano concerto, which moved me so strongly that I couldn't speak for a long time after it was over. Afterwards, Inna often invited me over, and we listened to works by other composers, and on Sundays we went to the Small Hall of the Moscow Conservatory where Conservatory students gave recitals. We sat in the upper gallery, where the tickets were free. There, over a period of two or three years, I heard most of the major classical works. For the performers, these were opportunities to perfect their art, and we young listeners were their most enthusiastic audience and their most sympathetic critics. Inna and I continued to go to these concerts long after we both moved away from our apartment building, and I have kept my love of classical music throughout my entire life.

This was so even though I had never seriously studied an instrument. When I was six, Mother arranged for a neighbor, a professional music teacher, to give me lessons. I went to their place twice a week and even did my homework there on days when I didn't have a lesson; they had a maid who let me in. I was an enthusiastic student, played the scales with gusto, never got tired and never missed a lesson.

That year, after the summer break was over, I went to see my teacher to arrange to continue lessons. I went on my own, without telling Mother; my parents, when they found out, laughed but didn't scold me. Unfortunately, my teacher had lost her eyesight as a result of a botched surgery and became completely blind. That was the end of my musical career but not the end of my love for music. I continued to listen to classical music on the radio and read everything I could about musicians and composers. I even gave a presentation in 9th grade, in Eduard Orestovich's literature class, on Sergei Prokofiev, a Russian-Soviet composer who had the misfortune to die on the same day as Joseph Stalin — March 5, 1953 — so that the anniversary of his death went unmarked and unmentioned for many years.

When Stalin began his crackdown on the arts, he didn't spare music. Dmitri Shostakovich's 9th Symphony* was singled out for harsh criticism. It was first performed in 1945, but I remember hearing it on the radio in my par-

---

* https://www.markwigglesworth.com/notes/marks-notes-on-shostakovich-symphony-nos-9-and-12/

ents' room and being deeply moved, moved beyond words. And I remember later hearing the official attacks on it on the same radio.

Other classical composers were also attacked, Sergei Prokofiev in particular. The newspapers accused his music of being too dark, too loud, of being anti-Soviet in style and essence. How could music itself—instrumental music without words—be anti-Soviet? What did these people know about music? But the regime wanted to control all of life, including all the higher, intellectual and aesthetic aspects of life, like literature, art, and music, which only added to the dark gray color of our existence.

During Khrushchev's Thaw, music, like other arts, went through something of a revival. Even before the 1957 Youth Festival, but especially after it, young people discovered jazz, finding in it a natural energy and freshness that rhymed with their own youthful energy and optimism. And in 1958, the first Tchaikovsky International Music Competition was held in Moscow. The American pianist Van Cliburn took first prize for his performance of Tchaikovsky's 1st Piano Concerto. We watched it on TV with our neighbors, whom we invited to join us because they didn't own a TV. Van Cliburn added a new level of emotion to this well-known piece, finding depths in it that we hadn't heard from domestic performers.

There was also a new genre that bridged the gap between music and poetry: singer-songwriters, known as "bards." Their songs, usually sung to the accompaniment of a single guitar, were fairly simple musically and often artlessly performed but carried lyrics charged with meaning that we all understood to represent a challenge to the regime, both political and aesthetic. They gave informal concerts that were recorded on reel-to-reel magnetic tape and later on cassette tapes; this unofficial method of distribution became known as magnitizdat.*

* * *

In 9th grade, I saw a student jazz band perform at a school party. Volodya Kotlyar played the guitar with gusto. Neither tall nor short, slender, with nice wavy hair and thoughtful eyes, clearly an intellectual, I had heard him described as very smart, intelligent and interesting. We knew each other to say hello in the hallway but never had an actual conversation. This went on for two years, during which his band performed a couple more times.

At the graduation party at the end of 10th grade, Volodya was one of the boys who asked me to dance. He was silent the whole time, which made him seem aloof; I was too young to recognize the defense mechanism of a nervous young man. For my part, I didn't mind too much: I had other people with whom I could dance and joke and laugh.

* * *

After graduation I took the entrance exam to the Pedagogical Institute (the Moscow teachers' college) but missed the passing grade by one point and went to work as a Young Pioneers team leader at a primary school. Young Pioneers was a middle-school feeder organization into the Communist Party (there were also Children of October for elementary-age students and the Komsomol, or Union of

---

* https://en.wikipedia.org/wiki/Magnitizdat

Communist Youth, for college students)*. My job was to organize political rallies and decorate the school for various revolutionary and other holidays. I quit that job at the end of the school year to focus on studying to retake the exam to teachers' college.

We lived close to Gorky Park, an amusement complex that was next to the venerable old park of Neskuchny Sad, which I liked better than all the rides with their loud music. The old park was nice because one could meander around in peace and quiet composing poetry or singing (or not), walk among tall, old trees, and gaze at the Moskva river from the high bank. Deep inside the old park, on a little hill, stood a cute little white and yellow two-story building, with balconies on both levels. It dated back to the 18th century, when it served as a tea house to the aristocratic Orlov family, but in my time it housed a public reading room where one could spend time reading books, leafing through magazines, or (as in my case) studying. On sunny days I liked to sit on the second-floor balcony. The reading room had a large collection of books and subscribed to all the popular literary magazines. It was run by two venerable silver-haired ladies, so ancient they might themselves have come from Count Orlov's time.

---

* https://en.wikipedia.org/wiki/Vladimir_Lenin_All-Union_Pioneer_Organization; https://en.wikipedia.org/wiki/Little_Octobrists; https://en.wikipedia.org/wiki/Komsomol

HELLO, VOLODYA...

One day, tired and hungry after several hours of studying, I decided to head home. On my way out of the park I stopped by some ping-pong tables to watch the games. One pair attracted my attention: a tall, blond, athletic young man with a confident economy of movement, and his partner, dark haired, shorter, with quick, nervous movements — they didn't seem evenly matched. I stood for a little while watching them, when suddenly (of course) the ball rolled toward my feet, and the shorter player ran to get it. It was Volodya Kotlyar. He recognized me a split second before I recognized him and greeted me with a surprising degree of enthusiasm: it emerged later that he had at first mistaken me for another girl he knew and then was happy to see that it was me and not her. We hadn't seen each other in a year and were naturally eager to hear what was going on in each other's life. Volodya set a date for a rematch with his friend, and he and I walked off together. Basically, we started talking and didn't stop until the last day of his life.

That day we talked for several hours, catching up on the basics. For example, I learned that Volodya got into the prestigious Foreign Language Institute — and placed straight into the second year! At that time, the Institute had set up a special experimental program for students whose foreign language proficiency exceeded the expected high school level. Volodya told me that his mother had found him an excellent French tutor, himself a graduate of the Institute, who got him excited not only about the language but also about the craft of translation, so that now Volodya was enrolled at the translation department and was studying simultaneous translation. I knew from my father that simultaneous translators were the elite, the *crème de la crème* of the profession.

The program excused the students from attending their first-year core curriculum classes and required them only to pass the exams in those subjects. Of the eleven freshmen, six dropped out after one semester, and only four finished the entire program. One of them was Volodya's blond ping-pong opponent, Zhenya Sidorov. But Volodya finished the program six months ahead of the others; he was eager to start working and earning money.

We walked all the way to the center of the city and continued along the Moskva river. I remember the zesty, exciting smell of chocolate wafting from the chocolate factory across the river.

Volodya told me about his parents. Both of them were architects by training, his father a lieutenant colonel in the army, his mother a homemaker taking care of her own mother, Volodya's grandmother, who lived with them. I told him about my parents. We exchanged the latest gossip about our former classmates and teachers. We talked about poetry, the latest important poems that had been published, about Khrushchev's recent meeting with a group of poets where he had scolded them for various political and aesthetic sins. We discovered that we liked the same poets, quoted the same books, and had the same sense of humor. Except that Volodya knew more, read more, and was fascinating to listen to. It was all so easy, so interesting—we didn't want to stop. But it was getting late, and both of us had to get home. We turned around and walked back; Volodya saw me to my tram stop and then went to take a trolleybus home.

* * *

From that day on, whenever we met, we continued right where we had left off. Sometimes he came to pick me up at the reading room, and we walked in the old park. Sometimes I took the metro to his Institute. When I got into my teachers' college, one stop over on the same metro line, we began to meet in the metro — either at his stop or mine. There, across the street from the metro, was an awful little eatery where we ate soggy meat-stuffed dumplings floating in watered-down sour cream. We ate our dumplings standing at tall round tables, much too tall for me, among rough working-class types who chuckled at my struggles and tried to find us room to sit down at one of the regular tables in the corners.

Afterwards, we went walking toward the center, eventually covering half of Moscow in our strolls. Volodya took me to his old stomping grounds in the historic center of Moscow, which he knew well, and showed me the buildings where major writers and other famous people had lived. He had spent his early years in that part of town before moving to Leninsky Prospect (to the same building where the "Synthetica" store was: how could I help but believe in fate after this?). Later on, we often walked along the Boulevard Ring, a string of wide, tree-shaded boulevards. That is where I first heard about the emerging artistic movement of the bards, not sanctioned or promoted by the state. Later I heard their songs, first as sung by Volodya, then in clandestine reel-to-reel tape recordings. Volodya often sang songs by Bulat Okudzhava, a bard and a writer, a man of the older generation who had fought in WWII and who more or less embodied the artistic conscience of the age. His songs, colored by the pain of his experience, were poignant, sincere and very sad.

Volodya also played the classical guitar, introducing me to a whole new kind of music I hadn't heard before. He was a big fan of the Spanish guitarist Andres Segovia. I learned about guitar composers such as Heitor Villa-Lobos and Francisco Tarrega; we attended concerts where their works were performed.

He infected me, and our friends, with his enthusiasm for the French language and culture. We thought French women the epitome of elegance, French cuisine the height of culinary art, etc. Volodya played his guitar and sang songs by Georges Brassens, Charles Aznavour and others. He let me listen to recordings of Gilbert Bécaud and Edith Piaf. This was during Khrushchev's Thaw, when foreign artists—including Aznavour, Yves Montand, etc—began coming to the USSR on tour. All the concerts were sold out, of course, but we were able to see some of them on TV—including one where Khruschev planted hearty Russian-style kisses on Yves Montand's face, embarrassing himself before the entire world.

* * *

Volodya took me to his Institute and showed me the audio room where simultaneous translators trained using special recording and playback devices called lingua-phones. He introduced me to another friend, Volodya Gerasimovich, a fellow translator who worked at the House of Friendship with Peoples of Foreign Countries, a cultural exchange and outreach organization, where he specialized in the Near East and had even visited Israel (a rare thing in those days) and had a lot of interesting things to say. He and his friends had formed a humorous "Society of Secret Tea-Totallers," whose members were supposedly non-drinkers at heart, but since everyone around them drank, so did they — to maintain appearances. They had an initiation ritual: a shot of vodka mixed with a pinch of black pepper, to be downed all in one gulp. When I got my breath back tears were streaming from my eyes, but I only grunted and laughed — to everyone's applause. I was in! These brilliant guys who did such amazing

Vladimir Kotlyar. *Moscow, 1964.*

things with words had accepted me as one of their own! I was flattered. When they got together and began swapping stories about translating errors and triumphs, it was as fascinating and as suspenseful as any hunting story.

This new friend also got my Volodya several gigs leading tours of foreign visitors for the House of Friendship. Volodya also led tours for the government's inbound tourism agency, Intourist. Another good thing about hanging around interpreters was that they were hired to provide Russian voice-overs for foreign movies at special closed screenings that were held for various VIPs — movies that were not shown in ordinary theaters. And the translators could get their friends into the screenings. I remember one such film, with Sophia Loren and Marcello Mastroianni, in which she complained to him that they were so poor that it had been two months since she'd bought a new pair of shoes. The audience hooted with laughter: Soviet people wore the same shoes for years on end.

* * *

Here is a story Volodya told me. Like many of his fellow students, he led tours of foreigners during summer vacation. Once, in 1964, he led a group of French Armenians, who were finally permitted under Khrushchev's Thaw to visit their relatives in Soviet Armenia. Volodya met them at the airport and took them to their hotel, where he asked everyone to stand next to their bags.

Volodya: "Has everyone found their bags?"
Armenians: "Yes, merci, monsieur."
V: "Has everyone received their room key?"
A: "Yes, merci, monsieur."
V: "Your room number is on the key. Has everyone found their room number?"
A: "Yes, merci, monsieur."
V: "You will now each receive a piece of chalk."
Volodya watches the concierge distribute pieces of chalk.
V: "Does everyone have a piece of chalk?"
A: "Yes, merci, monsieur."
They raise their pieces of chalk up.
V: "Now please use the chalk to write your room number on your bags so the porter can get the right bags to the right rooms. Okay?"
A: "Okay."

Each of the visitors then asked him to tell them again what they should do and why they should do it. So there stood my Volodya waiting for them to finish, when a tiny silver-haired lady came up to him and said: "Here, I did it!" — proudly handing him her piece of chalk... with her room number scratched into it with a pen. As they would say nowadays, facepalm.

* * *

The tour guides were issued lots of restaurant passes to feed their charges. They always had leftover passes, and Volodya once used them to invite me out to dinner. That was my first dinner out at a formal restaurant (as opposed to various cheap eateries and cafeterias). Restaurants were exclusive places, patronized by foreigners, Communist Party insiders, people with friends in high places, and the like. Ordinary intellectuals like my parents, untainted by such connections, made it a point of pride to stay away. But this was a date, so I went. The restaurant was called "Peking" and was located in the same building as the hotel of the same name for visiting foreigners, a tall, beautiful building in Mayakovsky Square. A large, spacious dining room with white napery, with few customers and (to my surprise) nothing Chinese about it at all: ordinary Russian waiters, classic Russian—albeit luxurious—food. I felt awkward and out of place but Volodya did his best to cheer me up. He ordered champagne, white bread and butter, and caviar, which was then inaccessible to mere mortals and not sold in stores. And nothing more. He wanted to make a gesture, to show off his worldliness and independence, and to treat me to something I couldn't have in everyday life. He forgot one thing, or actually, we both forgot it: I had never had champagne before, and any sparkling wine is metabolized very quickly, especially on an empty stomach, making the person very drunk.

I wouldn't recommend this to anyone. It was awful. I felt faint, my head was spinning, I had trouble staying upright. We left and set off walking; luckily, the weather was cool. At one point, Volodya had to prop me up against a tree because I couldn't walk, feeling really dizzy and nauseous. I had never been drunk before and had never felt so bad. We walked for a long time: I had to air my head out so my parents wouldn't realize I was drunk when I came home.

* * *

At the end of September of my first year of college, first-year students were sent to a *kolkhoz*, a Soviet collective farm, to help bring in the beet harvest. These agricultural interludes were a common part of the Soviet educational process and were used less for any educational benefit than as a source of free labor to the dysfunctional Soviet farming sector. We were housed on the campus of a summer camp, thirty girls in one big room. There was no privacy at all: we all washed, changed, slept together, and even used the toilet together, in a separate shed with no stalls, only a row of simple holes in the ground. After work, in the evenings, overwhelmed by the noise, I liked to get out of the dormitory just to have a bit of quiet time alone. One evening, someone realized that I wasn't there. They told the group leader, they called the police (*militsiya*), who brought their dogs out to search for me. Eventually I heard the dogs barking and came back; I hadn't even gone far, I was just strolling there among the trees near the dormitory. I got in trouble for my "antisocial individualism" and conceived a hearty loathing of all things collective.

* * *

1964. Khrushchev's Thaw was at an end. In Leningrad, the poet Iosif (Joseph) Brodsky was put on trial for "idleness", i.e., not having an official place of employment, which was a crime under Soviet criminal law; his writing was not deemed to be of sufficient merit to qualify as work. He was convicted, sentenced to five years hard labor and exiled to a remote village in the Arkhangelsk region in the north. His trial was a defining moment, not only in literature but also in journalism: the courageous author and journalist Frida Vigdorova made a transcript of the proceedings, which was later circulated clandestinely in typewritten copies. The trial was also attended by foreign media and was broadcast live on the BBC and the Voice of America; we listened to it as best we could on the radio, in between bursts of static from the Soviet jamming stations.

The trial also established another pattern: during the trial, Soviet media published letters from "the people" calling for the conviction of this "social parasite." Naturally, the authors of these screeds had never read a single one of Brodsky's poems.

Similar letters were published during the campaign against Aleksandr Solzhenitsyn after *The Gulag Archipelago* came out in the West. "I, Klavdiya Semenova, milkmaid at a collective farm," ran a typical letter, "have not read Solzhenitsyn's books, personally, but I agree with our Party and government leaders that such so-called writers have no place in our Socialist society. I and all the members of our collective farm write to express our condemnation of Comrade Solzhenitsyn."

Now anyone daring to say a good word about Solzhenitsyn or other disfavored poets, musicians or artists risked being accused of "anti-Soviet attitudes"—an increasingly actionable, and therefore dangerous, accusation.

* * *

Volodya and I continued to see each other. Sometimes we strolled around the Donskoy monastery, a walled compound dating back to the 16th century, which was located not far from my house. Along the outside of one high wall of dark-red brick ran a lovely alley shaded by tall, old trees and lined with benches that were always occupied by courting couples. On the other side there was a little open space, with its own trees and benches, used mostly by mothers and grandmothers with children. It was nice to walk there. It was there that, one day, I heard those quiet, momentous words that made my heart skip a beat. It took us both a little while to get used to being in love.

I remember walking past a fancy jewelry store in the center of Moscow and looking at the sparkling gems in the window. Volodya said he would like to buy me a diamond ring. Though neither of us had that kind of money and nothing came of it, the very words were a revelation: diamonds, to me, were for women that were quite out of my league; I owned no expensive clothes, and neither my mother nor any of our friends had any diamonds. Now I had someone who valued me enough to even imagine such a thing!

One day Volodya brought me home to meet his parents. I was very nervous, and his mother seemed nervous, too. When I sat down on the couch holding my little purse, she snatched it out of my hands, putting me even more off-balance; she told me later that she wanted to get it out of my way, to make me more comfortable. She was friendly, though, and asked about my parents, my classes. The tension quickly dissipated. Iraida Solomonovna turned out to be a short, heavy-set woman with quick, bird-like movements and a lovely sense of humor; she was easy to talk to. I could see how much Volodya took after her.

His father, Yakov Borisovich, a retired lieutenant colonel, had a much sterner demeanor and spoke and moved with a slow, ponderous dignity. He too proved to have a sense of humor despite his forbidding exterior. Volodya told me afterwards that they both liked me.

Sometimes we went to the movies; I always carried my ID, my internal passport, to get into movies rated for viewers over 16, since I was short and thin and looked younger than my age. We also went to the Central Lenin Library and spent hours there reading all kinds of interesting things. Volodya was an exceptionally fast reader (I had never met anyone who read as fast as he did) and had a retentive memory, which was how he was able to hold his own in conversations with all kinds of people, from scientists and techies to literary and humanities types. He was also a fascinating conversationalist.

And still we continued to walk and talk. And eventually told each other that we didn't want to be apart any longer but wanted to be together always, and therefore we should get married. There wasn't a formal proposal so much as an acknowledgment of a fact that was obvious to both of us, but for me this was the most romantic moment of my life.

Volodya was full of plans. We were going to live on his translator's wages and my teacher's salary, which should be enough for the two of us. Except that we had no place to live; at the time, most young couples moved in with their parents, but this wasn't an option for us. Volodya's family had no room for us because their apartment was only two rooms, one of which Volodya shared with his grandmother. I had a room of my own, as my brother was already living in a student dormitory at college, but my parents' apartment also consisted of only two rooms, and we would have to pass through my parents' room to get to mine. We decided to talk to our parents about helping us rent a separate apartment.

And that was when they poured cold water on our enthusiasm. They gave us an ultimatum: nineteen was too young for marriage, we should wait a year, and if we were still together then, we would get their full blessing and their help with finding a place and any other help we might need. Volodya's father was very strict.

But they couldn't break us. We knew that we were destined to be together, no matter what, and had a vision for our life together. Volodya continued to get assignments to translate written users' manuals for factory equipment, engines, some home appliances, etc., and delighted in reading aloud to me their Russian originals, which were sometimes so poorly written that it was hard to see how their intended audience—factory workers or housewives—could understand them. He continued to guide tours to other towns, making good money. And he called me as soon as he got home.

* * *

A year passed. One day we were walking down Griboyedov Street, home to the Griboyedov Wedding Palace, a beautiful, ornate 18th century building housing a marriage registrar office. "Let's go in," said Volodya. And just like that, as naturally as breathing, we went in and filled out an application and were given a wedding date of October 21—two months away. It was really happening; my heart skipped another beat. Even though we had talked about our shared future, Volodya didn't tell me in advance he intended to file that day but mentioned it only as we reached the place. We came out both feeling a little overwhelmed by the momentous step we had just taken. This was in August of 1965; I was about to start my third year at the teachers' college.

My parents were very happy, my father virtually glowed: they really liked Volodya. Even my brother Lyonya said something positive. And so our wedding preparations began: fabric was purchased and a wedding dress made, not by Miss Fanny this time but in a real dress shop; we ran around looking for white shoes for me. I rejected the veil as outdated and unfashionable and bought a silver hair clip. And Volodya's father dug in a drawer and brought out a massive, antique gold ring that had belonged to his mother. That ring made three good-size new rings: one for Yakov Borisovich himself, one for Volodya and one for me. That's how big it was.

I asked my mother to teach me to cook: the only recipe in my repertoire was eggs sunny side up. Mother taught me some of her signature dishes, which became my signature dishes: a great stew, and meatballs, and her salad, and many other things. Unfortunately, we didn't have much time, because my father was really sick: he had had two heart attacks on top of his diabetes and some other conditions and required a lot of attention.

* * *

During that time, my parents were having health problems. Father had been sick, on and off, for a very long time with diabetes and heart problems. Mother, who was his main caretaker, was exhausted both physically and mentally; she developed symptoms of depression and anxiety. None of us knew anything about mental health issues: I noticed that she was not well, but not right away, and even then I did not understand the extent of the problem. Eventually, Volodya's parents made an appointment for her with a psychiatrist, but Mother did not tell the doctor her most important symptoms because she thought that would make her sound "crazy": like most people at the time, she had a hard time admitting even to herself that she might need that kind of help. Untreated, the disease progressed to the point where it impacted her relationships with most of our family friends, including Aunt Maya Brin. There were no more holiday gatherings, no more "Maya's cake."

* * *

We all agreed that Volodya and I would rent our own separate room. This meant buying all the things necessary to set up our household. Iraida Solomonovna took me shopping for silverware and glasses; my mother helped me buy bed linens and other things.

Ten days before the wedding, my father was hospitalized with another heart attack, I wanted to postpone the wedding until Father recovered, and Volodya agreed. We went together to see Father at the hospital and told him our thoughts. But Father became very agitated and upset. The doctor came in and ordered us to stop upsetting him. Father calmed down a bit and said that he absolutely didn't want me to put my life on hold, and that he would celebrate with us when he was better. (He kept his word: after the wedding, when he was home and we came to visit, he raised a glass to our new life.)

* * *

Now Volodya and I had new things to talk about on our walks. I remember one walk where I said that we would have a daughter and would name her Masha (Maria). I liked everything about that name: its sweet, kind sound; its Biblical, universal flavor; and also its simplicity, which would protect her from the kinds of problems I had with my own name. I pictured our little Masha wearing a polka-dotted head scarf and playing in the sandbox with a little pail and shovel. However, after Masha was born, there were no polka-

Masha in polka dot scarf. 1973

dotted scarves to be found anywhere. Not in children's stores, not in women's stores, not even in fabric stores! There were pails and shovels but no scarves. They became available when Masha was three or four years old, and all our friends started bringing us polka-dotted scarves, with dots of all colors and sizes, from tiny pinpoints to huge circles, so big that only four or five fit on one scarf. Such were the unfathomable ways of a centrally planned economy.

* * *

On the morning of October 21, I took the tram to the hair salon and had my hair put up in a fashionable beehive updo. It was snowing lightly, the first flurries of the year, quickly carried away by the wind. Everyone went to the wedding palace. Yakov Borisovich had arranged for a photographer. In deference to his stern sense of propriety, not one of the pictures shows anyone hugging or kissing. I was very nervous, to the point of trembling, and was afraid the pictures might come out blurry, but they came out just fine.

Our Wedding. *October 21st, 1965*

Right after the ceremony we went to visit Father at the hospital, me still in my white dress and holding my wedding bouquet. All the doctors and nurses stopped by to congratulate us and give us their good wishes. Father was well enough to sit up and was delighted for us but I still felt a little guilty for not postponing the ceremony.

From there we went to see Volodya's grandmother, who was not well and had not attended our wedding. An unsentimental woman, she greeted us coolly but we knew she wished us well.

We had decided to have a small reception at my parents' place for just a few of our closest friends. Had Father not been ill, I still would not have wanted a big wedding with lots of guests. I have always felt that a wedding, when two people marry and begin their life together, was a very personal, intimate matter and didn't require a big, noisy affair.

Lyonya had picked the music; guests danced in both rooms and in the doorway between them. When they got tired of dancing, they went over to the table, where food — cooked by both our mothers and some of the girls — was laid out buffet-style. There were toasts and jokes and calls for the newlyweds to kiss, which was terrifying since our parents were right there... but we survived.

* * *

From there, alone at last, we went to our new place. For our first month, Yakov Borisovich had rented a studio apartment for us near the Gogol Theater: one large, sunny room, a white-tiled bathroom, a spacious kitchen — and all that just for us, with no neighbors to share with! There I took my first steps as a cook and homemaker. There was no telephone in the apartment (cell phones, of course, weren't even dreamed of) so I walked to a pay phone outside the theater when I needed to call someone. For example, when Volodya went away on tour with his French delegation and was out of town for several days, I was required to call his parents every evening after work; it was a little scary to walk down the dark, deserted street.

For the next two years we rented rooms in various apartments. Our last landlady, Maria Vasilyevna, deserves a special mention. She and her sister lived in a two-room apartment and rented out one of the rooms, a tiny, 7 sq. m. (75 sq. ft) room with a narrow metal-frame bed, a wardrobe, a small desk and two chairs. In order to fit in the bed together, we put our suitcases between the bed and the wall: that solved the width issue, but we could feel the handles poking up even through a layer of blankets. We lived like that for over a year and managed just fine.

Maria Vasilyevna was nice to us; she liked me because I treated her with respect and because I had a good relationship with my mother-in-law (especially since she herself didn't get along with her daughter-in-law). A professional chef, she shared with me several cooking secrets and general household tips and tricks. I was a grateful student. One day I made a stew, using techniques I had learned from her and from my mother and mother-in-law, and was amazed to find that it tasted good. "Of course it tastes good," laughed Maria Vasilyevna, "better than axe soup*, I reckon."

We. 1965

We were the only couple among all our friends who had our own place, and they often came over. Maria Vasilyevna was very tolerant of our late-night get-togethers. I fried slices of bologna, which curved up in the hot skillet, forming little concave shapes into which I spooned canned green peas, with golden home fries on the side. It made for a pretty presentation. We would eat holding our plates in

* https://en.wikipedia.org/wiki/Stone_Soup

78

our laps or on each other's shoulders, since there was no-where else to set them on. This gave rise to my reputation as a cook: now I really had to learn! Even after we had left Maria Vasilyevna, our friends continued to come over, and I liked to feed them, showing off my new skills. Volodya played his guitar and sang, and everyone sang along. We all had a good time.

In the mornings Volodya and I walked to the metro to-gether to go to our respective schools. In the winter, the snow was higher than I was tall, and groundskeepers cut pathways through the snow with their shovels so people could get from the building entrance to the street. We walked down those paths as though down white-walled hallways. It was fun!

We stayed with Maria Vasilyevna for almost a year, un-til Yakov Borisovich got us our own separate two-room cooperative apartment in the new suburb of Matveyevs-koye, in the southwest part of Moscow. Both sets of parents helped us make payments on it for the first year and a half. Volodya graduated from college six months before I did and got a job right away, and we gratefully declined their help from that point on. Volodya felt that providing for our family was his responsibility and was happy to be able to relieve our parents of that burden.

* * *

1967. After graduating from the teachers' college, I got a job at a school teaching Russian language and litera-ture to 5th through 8th grades. On the first day of classes, I wrote out my full name—Zhanneta Genrikhovna—on the blackboard in chalk, and one of my students asked me:

"How come you're so little, and your name is so long?" Everyone laughed, including me.

My job involved five solid hours of talking, six days a week. By the end of the first month I had lost my voice: in the third period I could still speak, albeit in a hoarse voice, but by the 4th period I could only whisper and write out the instructions on the board. My students found it hilarious but kept quiet so as not to attract attention.

And so it happened that I was at home on sick leave, when my brother Lyonya called to say that Father had passed away — at the hospital, from a heart attack, his fourth. I ran to be with Mother. A few days later, Father's body was cremated and interred at the columbarium at the Donskoy monastery. Strangely, I could not weep; I felt a black emptiness inside and didn't want to talk to anyone. My heart ached for Mother, everything felt strange, but the tears refused to come.

A few months after Father's death, Volodya and I went to the theater to see "Dear Liar", a play by Jerome Kilty (translated into Russian) based on the correspondence between Bernard Shaw and the actress Stella Patrick Campbell. A great Russian actor, Rostislav Platt, played Bernard Shaw; he seemed on the verge of tears when he read one of Shaw' letters that describes his mother's death and cremation. I fell apart right there in my seat. All the tension of the last few months, all my grief for my father poured out in those tears, and I could not stop weeping. I had to leave the show; Volodya left with me. And for some time afterwards I cried for the most trivial reasons, until my grief lifted a little and I felt more like myself again.

* * *

August 1968. We spent the summer at Mukachevo, a little town in the Carpathian mountains. A pretty little town, with an ancient monastery high on the side of the mountain. The landlady rented out rooms to two other couples. The landlady, a robust, cheerful woman named Yulia, put her hands on her hips and declared that "scrawny little girls don't live long," and therefore she must fatten me up. She wasn't the first, alas; all my life people have tried to fatten me up. Yulia got her neighbor to bring me fresh goat milk every morning, since it was so good for my health. Interestingly, I did gain a little weight and then didn't get sick all winter.

One sunny day we were taking one of our walks in town when we saw silent, sullen crowds lining the street and tanks rolling down the middle, dark-green monsters that seemed to take up the whole street. These were Soviet invasion forces on their way to Czechoslovakia to put down the Prague Spring* and to depose the Czech leader, the reformer Alexander Dubček.

* * *

At that time—late 1960s and into the 1970s and beyond—the government re-established strict control over literature and art. Gone were the poetry readings in Mayakovsky Square. Pushed out of the public domain, independent poetry and prose went underground, where they flourished, unhampered by censorship. Courageous individuals made copies of these illegal works by re-typing them on manual typewriters over carbon paper, several copies at a time.

---

* https://en.wikipedia.org/wiki/Prague_Spring

Most of the time they worked at someone else's *dachas*, out in the country, where the sound of the typewriter wouldn't be picked up by neighbors' ears. These copies were circulated from hand to hand. This was called *samizdat*—from the Russian words for "self" and "published": the original self-publishing. That is how I came to read the memoirs of Nadezhda Mandelshtam about her husband, the great Russian poet Ossip Mandelshtam, who had perished in the Gulag, arrested for a poem about Stalin.

> *We live without feeling our country's pulse,*
> *We can't hear ourselves, no one hears us,*
> *If a word is uttered by chance,*
> *The Kremlin Highlander is remembered at once*.*

We were given an evening, two at most, to read each illegal copy, both because the next reader was waiting and because it was dangerous to keep such papers at home: no one knew at whose home "they" might show up next with a search warrant. In the same way, we read Solzhenitsyn's *Cancer Ward*, whose protagonist, a patient in a cancer ward, reads an order in a newspaper announcing the rehabilitation of the Gulag prisoners and is terrified that those of them who owed their imprisonment to his secret reports will find him and beat him to a pulp. The informer feared the impending retribution more than his fatal illness.

There were also publishing houses set up abroad to bring out banned Russian books, or other books in Russian translations. They also published literary magazines that printed essays, short stories, and poetry. This litera-

---

* Translated by Ian Probstein. https://jacket2.org/commentary/ian-probstein-mandelstam-stalin-epigram

ture—not self-published but published "over there"—was dubbed *tamizdat* and smuggled back into Russia. Years later, in 1986, I would read *tamizdat* editions of George Orwell's *Animal Farm* and *1984* and would be stunned to find a book written 37 years prior that so accurately described our current reality, down to the smallest details.

Exposed to this new writing, young intellectuals—especially scientists and engineers, trained to some degree in rigorous habits of mind—came to discern the difference between propaganda and reality. These began to coalesce into a quasi-opposition movement of political dissenters, or "dissidents." *

Another quasi-literary genre that blossomed during the dissident period was the phenomenon of *anekdot*, or a suggestive joke with a political subtext. For example, there was one about the Soviet Premier, Leonid Brezhnev, who was walking down the street and saw a man walking toward him, carrying a watermelon. "What a nice-looking watermelon," says Brezhnev. The man lifts his watermelon toward him and says: "Here, you choose." "What's there to choose?" says Brezhnev, "you only have one watermelon." "We only have one you," says the man, "and yet we choose you in every election."

* * *

After graduation, Volodya got a job with a publishing house that published military and technical books in foreign translations. Most of the staff were civilians or retired military, but the publishing house—like all Soviet employ-

---

* https://en.wikipedia.org/wiki/Soviet_dissidents

ers—had a security desk in their HR department. The desk was headed by an active duty colonel, probably with the KGB, who once said at a staff meeting that the chief enemies of the state were "Jews, college students, and people who spoke foreign languages." My Volodya fit that profile perfectly: he was Jewish, a former university student, and he spoke two foreign languages, French and English—and had a mother-in-law who was an American, which was even worse. And these words were uttered not in 1937, not in 1953, but in 1971!

In the meantime, I was pregnant. Everyone who saw me thought I was carrying a boy, but I told everyone that it was a girl. If God or nature had had any doubts, I guess I finally convinced them, because on August 14, 1970 I gave birth to our daughter Masha.

I don't remember who gave me a book by Dr. Benjamin Spock, *Baby and Child Care*. I became so completely engrossed in it that I could hardly put it down all through my pregnancy. I had never been around newborns, had never even seen one up close before, and so this book was a tremendous help to me in my daily life with the baby. Dr. Spock's main advice—that parents should trust their common sense—fascinated me, especially in the prescriptive and authoritarian Russian environment. Such a simple idea, but it helps so much, even now, years later.

While we waited, we both felt that a baby, even one still in the womb, should "see" beauty and "hear" good music, so we went to the Tretyakov Art Gallery and to classical concerts. I particularly remember hearing Paganini's music for violin and guitar, performed by prominent Russian musicians Victor Feliciant and Natalia Ivanova-Kramskaya at the Moscow Municipal Library of Foreign-Language Literature. It was a magical evening, and I was sure that my little girl was enjoying it. Coincidentally, our daughter has loved classical music, including classical guitar, since childhood. We began taking her to classical concerts fairly early.

The day Masha was born, Volodya was in Leningrad working as an interpreter at an international symposium. "As far as I know," he told his colleagues, "I have no children"; he was off by a couple of hours. He first saw our daughter through the window of the maternity hospital, since visitors were not allowed. Seeing her tightly swaddled in her little cocoon, he agreed that she was a true Masha, and no other name would do. When we brought her home, he carried her all around our apartment, showing her the rooms, and the closets, and the kitchen...

Both our mothers helped out. Volodya's mother brought us meals; my mother came to help with the laundry or take the baby out for a walk so I could take a nap, as the baby was keeping me up at night.

One day Volodya's mother ran into our last landlady, Maria Vasilyevna, and told her that we had a daughter named Maria (Masha). Maria Vasilyevna was very touched, assuming that we had named our daughter in her honor. We hadn't, really, but no one had the heart to tell her. Masha was a very popular name, and there were a lot of Mashas around,

With my baby
daughter Masha
October 1970

85

like our dear Big Masha who was with us on our last day as we left for America.

I remember when Masha was four or five months old, I was watching TV while nursing her; Volodya was at work. The TV anchor, looking grim, announced that global cooling was upon us, the Arctic Ocean was on the brink of freezing over, and soon the whole Earth would freeze. I looked at Masha and asked her, in all seriousness, what we were going to do — or maybe the crisis would hold off until she grew up? And suddenly my little baby gave a happy giggle, maybe even her first, making me laugh too. Thankfully, the global cooling didn't materialize, the Earth didn't freeze, and we all survived. God willing, global warming will spare us also...

* * *

On December 31, 1970 my childhood friend Marina from Leningrad, now Saint Petersburg, came to help us celebrate Masha's first New Year's. Marina told us about a new and growing grassroots movement of young Jews in Leningrad seeking the right to emigrate from the Soviet Union. We knew of a similar movement in Moscow but until then we had never had an in-depth talk with anyone about it. This gave us a lot to think about, although we didn't make any decisions for several years yet.

* * *

One day in January of 1971, when Masha was five months old, my mother came by to tell me that Lyonya was planning to come see me. He had gone to the OVIR and would come straight from there. "Great," I said, "what's the occasion? And what is the OVIR?" And that's when Mother told me that she and Lyonya were leaving the country for good to move to the U.S, and that the OVIR was a visa office where he had gone to collect their exit visas. She told me that Lyonya was active in the civil rights movement, that he was involved in several causes, including the right of free emigration for Soviet Jews, and also that he had worked with the U.S. embassy in Moscow, which had helped him force the Soviet government to recognize the validity of his U.S. citizenship. She told me many other things about his activities that I had never known.

All this, coming out of the blue, shook me to the core. Why had they told me none of these things before? How could they have kept this from me?

Mother replied that she hadn't wanted to upset me because I was nursing, and stress was bad for a nursing mother. Volodya thought they had been afraid to tell me because of our military connection: Volodya's father was a retired army lieutenant colonel, and Volodya himself was working for a military publisher.

This conversation happened in January; they had a flight booked, leaving in February. I was told to come to Mother's place to collect some things I might want to keep.

When I arrived, some friends of Lyonya's were already there asking for this and that, it was noisy and distracting. I felt out of place, as though I were intruding. Mother was at home but we couldn't really talk in all that commotion, although she found a moment to give me 3,000 rubles that she had put aside for me.

She came to see me once or twice after that, but it was painful each time. And then she came one last time to say goodbye. She told me that Lyonya didn't want me to come to the airport to see them off because it might be dangerous: the place would be crawling with the KGB, who were watching him because of his civil rights activities, and he wanted to keep me out of it.

And then they were gone. Father had already been gone, and now so were my mother and brother. I had no more family left. I felt abandoned, excluded, betrayed. Nothing but empty bitterness. It was February 20, 1971.

I could not get over it for months. I kept having long mental conversations with my mother, telling her why they shouldn't have done this to me. I cried a lot. Volodya hovered over me, urging me to stop crying so my negative emotions wouldn't pass to our daughter through my milk. At other times he let me cry it out, scream it out, pour all my grief out. But the grief refused to leave. I blamed my brother, I blamed my Jewishness, I was in despair. Had they told me sooner, had they shared their reasons with me, I might not have taken it so hard. I might even have understood and accepted Mother's wish to live out the rest of her life in America, where she had her roots, where she still had family living. If only they had told me...

But then came the day when I wiped my tears, washed my face, put some makeup on, powdered my nose and decided: that's enough! I'll be OK. We'll be OK. After all, Mother herself had lived all alone in the Soviet Union for 40 years, with no parents or extended family around. And I am just as strong, I thought, and I have Volodya, and we have our little Masha, so sweet and trusting and so mine! And I would never leave her. She needs a stable, emotionally present mother. It was time for me to get back to my main job: being her mother.

Thankfully, years later, when I was working on this memoir, I was able to meet with Lyonya and talk this over.

He heard me out and understood me and agreed that I should write about all this here. What a blessing that this painful episode is finally healed and closed.

In the meantime, we spent Mother's 3,000 rubles to buy our first car: a *Zaporozhets*, a little Soviet-made clunker. Owning a car was one of Volodya's dreams, and we were happy enough with our little clunker, even though some of our friends who had well-connected parents owned better vehicles. Of course, in the Soviet Union everything related to cars — getting fuel, spare parts, inspection, tuning, repair — was so expensive, complicated and painful that we sold our car three years later.

* * *

We started getting occasional letters from Mother in the U.S. that she sent with visitors traveling to the Soviet Union, as none of us trusted the postal service. Sometimes the visitors also brought little presents from Mother.

But I hadn't fully understood all the repercussions of Mother and Lyonya's departure. The Iron Curtain was not merely a political reality: it was also in people's minds. In the fortress mentality that prevailed around us, leaving the country was treason, moral dereliction, especially leaving in order to move to the chief ideological adversary — the United States. And it reflected directly on the remaining family members, on us, who were immediately cast as unreliable, undesirable, even ideologically contagious. I had trouble finding a job. Volodya's parents, especially his mother, took it very hard; it was a good thing that his father was already retired, so it couldn't hurt him at work.

* * *

Volodya was forced to quit his job. In order to support us, he started doing freelance work at home, translating books on higher math, cybernetics and physics into French. Before starting work on each new book, Volodya did a lot of reading to master the subject—he called it "wallowing in the subject"—and telling me all about it, which I found fascinating. It was amazing to see him, a quintessential liberal arts type, master the nuances of technical disciplines. Besides his written work, he resumed his simultaneous translation at all kinds of international conferences held in other cities (all within the Soviet Union, of course).

Once, when Volodya was away, the doorbell rang. A *militsiya* man (a policeman) barged in and plopped down in our overstuffed chair in the living room as though he owned the place; the idea that one might refuse to let a policeman in without a warrant was unknown in the Soviet Union. He began asking me questions about Volodya's work, and how it was that he wasn't on any official payroll anywhere, and was he really working. These were not innocent questions: "idleness" was an actual crime under Soviet law. I said that my husband was a contract translator and was away working at an international symposium out of town. The policeman, a young man, had made himself comfortable in our chair and was even trying to flirt with me a little, when my wonderful three-year-old daughter, with perfect timing, came up to me and asked, looking at him with her large green eyes: "Mama, when is this man going to leave?" And the man finally realized that he had overstayed his welcome and got up to leave.

* * *

I stayed home with Masha for the first three years, tutoring high school students who were preparing for their college entrance exams, and helping them write their essays. Later, when she started preschool, I took typing classes and began to take in work, although I never reached my mother's speed.

Then I began to look for regular employment. Teaching school was no longer a viable career: no school system would hire me with my mother living in America. So I got a job as a proofreader at a legal publishing house, which lasted until they found out about my mother. I applied to different places, but parents' information was requested on application forms everywhere. So, too, was "nationality" (ethnicity). The Soviet Union classified Jewishness as an ethnicity, not a religion, and discriminated against Jews in every sphere of life, from hiring to promotion to every conceivable benefit. The entry for "nationality" was number five on all the standard application forms, and our friends often joked that someone was not hired or was denied permission to go on a business trip abroad because he was "lame in his fifth leg," i.e., Jewish. So I had two strikes against me, and I rarely got past the hiring department.

I caught a glimmer of hope at one agency where the head of the editorial department I was applying to interviewed me in person. She seemed well-disposed toward me, praised my wide reading and intellectual background, and asked me to call back at the end of the day, at 5:45 pm precisely. I stood by the pay phone for several minutes, afraid to call too early. When I called, I was told that the lady had left for the day 15 minutes previously and was leaving on a month-long vacation in the morning. And no, she didn't leave any instructions about me. So that was that.

A neighbor of ours, the father of one of Masha's little friends from our building, a Russian man named Yura Zaitsev, decided to try and help me. He worked at a space research institute, had heard that their publishing department needed an editor, and said he would talk to them about me. Volodya tried to talk him out of it but Yura would not be deterred. He came to see us the next day with eyes the size of saucers. The department head had told him openly that they had already "filled their Jewish quota." Poor Yura was so embarrassed it was painful to look at him.

Someone else told me that the Institute of Oriental Studies didn't ask about parents on their application form for secretaries, so I applied for a secretarial/typist position at their Middle East literature department and got a job that paid 90 rubles a month. What joy!

The department employed some very interesting people, experts on Asian and Near Eastern countries. I typed up their articles, answered the phone, and was in the office every day—unlike the rest of them, who came to the office twice a week. Once I was even tasked with distributing the payroll for the month; I received a thick wad of bills at the finance department, along with a ledger, signed for it there, brought it to our room and handed out the amount due to each employee, and they, too, signed the ledger to confirm receipt. I also was in charge of the office supplies closet, which was kept locked; when I was interviewing for the job, I heard my predecessor tell people—writers, who needed paper to work—that she could not give out too much paper to any one person ("into one pair of hands") because the nation was experiencing a "paper shortage": a petty tyrant wielding arbitrary power. I made sure to never do anything like that.

I worked there for a year and got along wonderfully with everyone. I enjoyed spending time around these remarkable people, hearing them tell fascinating things about "their" countries. For example, I heard about the Iranian revolution and the ascent of the Ayatollah Khomeini—and heard that the Shah Mohammad Reza Pahlavi, whom Khomeini overthrew, had been a highly educated man who protected women's rights.

At the end of the year, I got a substantial raise—my salary went up to 110 rubles a month. Having worked for a year, I was also eligible for a vacation, so I decided to spend it visiting my mother in America. Under the rules of the day, this required my employer's permission. And that's when all hell broke loose. The HR manager yelled at me at the top of her shrill voice; she called in the head of my department, a prominent professor, an expert in Indian studies. They continued to berate me together (although the professor, an educated man with polished manners, never raised his voice). How had I dared not to tell them that my mother was in America? I said: "Your application form didn't ask about parents." The HR manager said, indignantly: "And to think that she did a good job, that we gave her a raise!" I found it deliciously ironic to be accused of doing a good job: this was the nicest accusation I have ever received!

They fired me, effective at the end of the month. In the few remaining days, the attitude of the staff toward me underwent a drastic change. Most of them steered well clear of me: one might think they were afraid of catching an ideological infection. One of them, a prominent expert in Chinese studies, who translated Chinese poetry and was also the head of our department's Communist Party cell, said to me in a condescending tone:

Masha in 1st grade. *Moscow*

"Zhanna, my dear, I'm sure you understand the problem. You say you want to go visit your mother, but what if you decide to stay there, in the West?"

"But I'm leaving my husband and my six-year-old child here!"

"Ah, but I'm sure you realize that you can get your child back with no problem at all through international family courts. As for your husband... we all know that husbands are easily replaceable these days."

I looked at him with such horror that he let out an embarrassed giggle and walked away.

I had lost my job, and yet I was not allowed to leave the country. It was a bitter pill to swallow.

* * *

In August, 1977, Masha turned seven, and in September, she started school. We had met a couple of teachers of French through Volodya's college friends, and one of them taught at a primary school that offered intensive French instruction and was within a short bus ride from our home. We became friends with that teacher and her husband and at their recommendation enrolled Masha at the school where they both taught. French classes began in second grade, three years earlier than in regular schools. Masha excelled in the language.

I love cooking!
Moscow, 1987

One day, a few months into the school year, I walked into the living room, where Volodya and Masha sat awaiting dinner. I began to say something, but Volodya spread his hands wide and made a puzzled face, as though he couldn't understand what I said. He turned to Masha, signaling that she should translate my words into French for him, as best she could, using whatever vocabulary she then possessed — and translate his answers back into Russian for me. Thus began one of our favorite games that continued for several years.

* * *

The 1970s in the Soviet Union saw the growth of political dissent and the start of civil rights movement. There were street protests and demonstrations calling for the right of Soviet Jews to emigrate and move to Israel, their historical homeland. Some of our friends took part in the protests. Some of those who had applied to emigrate were allowed to do so if they showed a formal invitation from relatives residing in Israel. Some of these invitations were genuine and came from long-lost family members in Israel, but alongside those a small cottage industry grew up manufacturing fictitious relatives and invitations.

However, most of the applications were denied: the government refused to grant them, which gave rise to the term *refusenik*. These *refuseniks* included prominent mathematicians, physicists and other scientists. Among them was a young engineer from Donetsk Natan (Anatoly) Scharansky who became a leading activist in the Jewish movement, was arrested and imprisoned on fabricated charges of espionage and subversive activity, and after his release and repatriation to Israel became a prominent Israeli politician and member of government.

Our friends now talked a lot about emigration applications filed and denied, about street protests and demonstrations, about the KGB wiretapping people's phones. Eventually, Volodya and I also made a decision to emigrate. We had had enough of a life lived in whispers, of looking over our shoulders to avoid eavesdroppers, of looking for out-of-the-way pay phones when we wanted to make a private call to a friend. Many of our friends had already filed their applications.

In October 1979 we went to the OVIR and applied for permission to emigrate to America. But on December 25 of that year, Soviet forces invaded Afghanistan. We heard about it on the evening news. I was in another room when I heard Volodya exclaim loudly: "What are you doing, you bastards!" I ran in, and Volodya told me what was going on. Like everything else in Soviet politics, whether domestic or foreign, this had an impact on the "Jewish question." Our application apparently went into a deep freeze: a year passed before we heard back from the OVIR, and when we did, it was a denial. We became *refuseniks*.

We continued to apply for two or three years afterwards and then stopped. Some of our friends who were also trying to get out were in the same boat: some were kept waiting for a year, others for two years or longer. People rarely knew the true reasons for the denial, though oftentimes they were told it had to do with "state secrets" they had purportedly had access to. Volodya, for example, had had an actual security clearance, so we had somewhat expected a denial, but some of our friends were denied even though they had had nothing to do with security clearance or state secrets. A community of *refuseniks* was emerging.

Our relationships were also changing. Some of our old friendships cooled, as our friends now felt uncomfortable associating with us. Others, conversely, became even closer. My dear Zhenya stayed with me to the end, even though we had to resort to that payphone routine to speak with one another.

* * *

As the Soviet Jews as a group were maturing and becoming self-aware through their shared struggle for the right of emigration, this period also brought about a shift in my own self-identity. I reevaluated my own history, came to own my Jewishness, stopped feeling like a pariah and generally began to hold my head high.

I forgave my mother. I came to realize how hard it must have been for her as a young woman to leave behind her good, tight-knit Jewish family, her comfortable American life, only to find herself mired in this Soviet waking nightmare, this dark gray life... Years later, I saw a film that portrayed exactly that: *East/West* by Regis Wargnier*. My parents had their friends and could talk to them about the

---

* https://en.wikipedia.org/wiki/East/West

Michael family:
Jacob Michael first on the left.
Esther Michael last on the right.
Bronx, USA, 1930s

oppressiveness of Soviet life. But they had no family. They couldn't even write to their relatives abroad, so dangerous it was—on both sides, really: here, in the USSR, it could get them arrested, but even in America, during the McCarthy era, my mother's brother Lou, who at one point worked as a schoolteacher, was afraid of losing his job because of his "foreign connections." Letters got lost in the mail and were opened and read by government censors anyway. The rare Westerners who came to the USSR, bringing letters from her American family, tended to be naïve believers in the imaginary glories of socialism, while Mother and others like her were trapped in the real socialism, the dark gray socialism of scarcity, fear and oppression.

I thought also of my brother Lyonya, who was now free. In America, he was able to complete his education, get a degree in computer programming and get a job at a big company—all of it without worrying about "Jewish quotas." No one persecuted him for being a Jew, for attending a synagogue.

During our *refusenik* period, Volodya continued his translation work in order to support us. Since this was

Standing: Lady guest from US.
Sitting: Leonid, Esther, Janet,
Henry Rigerman.
Moscow 1959–1960

long before personal computers, he used his typewriter, but the typewriter could not handle complicated mathematical formulas, so I would cut them out of the original book and paste them into the typescript. When Volodya found errors in his translation, he typed the correct words on a clean sheet of paper, and I cut out the words or even single characters and pasted them over the error in the typescript. It was a long process that required careful attention but it was still faster than re-typing the whole page because of a typo. Volodya praised me for my good work, he said he himself could never do such a neat job. And I was glad that I could help.

He also continued to travel to conferences and symposia. These paid well: after one three-day conference, he made enough money to buy me a good winter coat and boots, which kept me warm for several years.

* * *

After Mother and Lyonya left, I lost touch with all of their friends, including Aunt Maya Brin—until, one day, her son Misha Brin walked back into my life. Literally. Through my front door.

A friend of Volodya's called to ask if Volodya might help a friend of his, a mathematician who was looking to do some English translation on the side, by the name of Misha Brin.

Brin! and a mathematician! this couldn't be a mere coincidence!

Volodya invited the man over, telling me to stay out of sight until their business was done. Of course, I found a reason to peek out from the kitchen when Volodya went to let him in. I didn't recognize Misha, but when we sat down to dinner he said he had recognized me right away — without needing to see our old childhood pictures from our summers in Anapa that I had prepared to show him.

Misha told us he was married; his wife's name was Zhenya; they had a six-year-old son, Seryozha (Sergey); they lived with Aunt Maya. He invited me over, and when I went to see them, Aunt Maya told me about Mother's mental health problems that had caused their estrangement. I was delighted to renew our friendship after all those years.

* * *

January 1983. I woke up in the middle of the night with a panic attack, sensing that something was wrong with my mother. I went to the kitchen to call my brother in New York but could not reach him, could not understand what the voice on the other end of the phone line was saying. In the morning, I called Boris Lempert, an old friend of my father's still living in Moscow and a native English speaker. He offered to meet me at the Central Post Office in Gorkiy Street (now restored to its pre-Communist name of Tverskaya) and to make the call for me, to speak with American phone operators and explain the problem and get them to connect me. It had to be in the evening because of the time zone difference. It worked, we got through and I learned that Mother was in the hospital, with cancer, and had been operated on the day before—at the precise time when I woke up.

Boris suggested getting Lyonya to send me a telegram from Mother's hospital: perhaps a telegram stating her condition would help me get the government permission to leave, to go see her, despite our *refusenik* status. I hadn't seen her in 12 years; all I had were infrequent phone calls and occasional letters and presents brought by foreign visitors.

Thus began my bureaucratic odyssey. I received the telegram fairly quickly, within a day or two. It said that Mother had been diagnosed with colon cancer and had two months left to live. I went to the OVIR and sat in line for a long time. Then I saw two women carrying enormous stacks of files, so tall that the women had to lean backwards a bit to balance them.

Soon after that, I was told to go in. I came in and saw a desk with the files piled on top of it and realized that all these files were my brother's case files.

Behind the desk sat a large, imposing man holding one of the files.

"Your application says you want to go to America to see your mother. Remind me how your mother came to be in America?"

"She was born there, she came to the Soviet Union in 1931 and went back in 1971."

"Is she a Jew?"

"Yes."

"Did she ever apply to emigrate to Israel? There are many people these days who lie to us, you know, they apply to go to Israel but end up in America."

"My mother never lied to anyone and never tried to go to Israel. She left because her father was dying and she wanted to see him while he was still alive. And that's what I'm trying to do, too, because she is dying."

"You want to go alone?"

"Yes."

"So, you say you want to go to New York. Alone. Not on a business trip and not as part of an organized tour group." (He meant that I would be outside of the field of vision of the undercover KGB agents who always accompanied business travelers and tourist groups.) "We'll have no way of knowing what you might do, will we? You could say you were going to New York but end up—oh, I don't know—in Chicago!"

I stared at him, uncomprehending, and he told me to go back to the waiting room. Some time later, a secretary came out and told me to go home; they would call me.

I went home and waited for a long time. I was on pins and needles: the first month of the two was almost over. The dear Boris Lempert came to my aid again: he suggested I go straight to the top and call the Office of The First Secretary of the Central Committee of the Communist Party. I should call precisely at 9:15 am. Office hours started at nine; I should give the man five minutes to hang up his coat and check his schedule, ten minutes to look through his inbox, leaving fifteen minutes free before his first meeting of the day. I called right on time and got through to the First Assistant of the First Secretary. I gave him my name and told him that my mother had repatriated to America (and had never tried to deceive the Soviet government); she was terminally ill; I wanted to go visit her; my husband and child would stay behind.

The Party Official took it all down and said he would look into it and someone would call me back. They called me from the OVIR two days later and gave me an appointment for next Wednesday at 11 a.m. in Room 22.

"But the OVIR is closed to the public on Wednesdays?"

"You must come. Someone will let you in."

Room 22 was known among *refuseniks* as the "rejection room." I spent the intervening days in a fog of worry. Volodya tried to comfort me by saying that they wouldn't call me in during off hours just to hand me a rejection, so it must be positive.

I went. They let me in. There was no one else in the waiting room. A woman with blank, expressionless eyes invited me into Room 22 and handed me an instruction booklet detailing a Soviet citizen's rules of conduct while abroad. For example, if I were riding a train while abroad and found myself in a compartment with a person of the opposite sex, I must demand to be moved to a compartment with a person of the same sex. There were many other oddities, like the prohibition on the "possession, sale or exchange of pearls"—just pearls, no diamonds or other gems—"whether loose or in jewelry settings." I had never even seen actual pearls, whether loose or in settings. Who could have thought that mere twenty-five years later I would be free to buy loose pearls, set them myself and sell my jewelry creations, all completely legally? But that would be in another life.

The woman handed me a stack of official forms, including a permission to buy a one-way ticket to the United

States and a permission to receive 120 USD cash in accordance with the then-current official exchange rate. She warned me that this was not enough money to buy a round-trip ticket, and that my relatives in the U.S. must buy my return ticket. She also told me the next steps, which involved going to more bureaucratic organizations and getting more forms and signatures. It was all a big hassle but it had to be done — and so it was done. At the bank I got the dollars, which I was seeing for the first time, and was surprised to see that the bills of different denominations were all the same color and size, unlike the multi-colored Russian paper money. I was unsure how I would tell them apart when it came time to pay but hoped I would manage, and in the event, I did.

In My Pearls

Volodya and Masha came to the Sheremetyevo airport to see me off. The small indignities of Soviet life were present there, as everywhere else: the customs people opened my bags and pawed through everything, including my underwear: take that, you nobody, who presumes to go to America!

It is hard to convey the emotion I felt during that whole process of check-in and departure. I had never traveled alone, I had never crossed the Soviet border — and now I was about to do so — and to go to America, the most forbidden, the most impossible of all places!

There were no direct flights from Moscow to New York but there was one from Montreal so I had to change planes in Montreal. I was on my way!

* * *

At the Montreal airport, I had an hour between flights and needed to find a restroom but didn't see (or couldn't understand) the signs for one. I tried to follow my nose— a fail-safe method back home—but detected no tell-tale stench. A woman, noticing my dismay, addressed me in English and pointed me to the right place. My God, what was this place? A large, pleasant, spotless room, well-lit mirrors, metal chairs with white leather seats, with sweet-smelling flowers in little vases on top of marble counters. Truly a room that conjured up a sense of restfulness. That was my first culture shock in the West.

Next step: to find my flight. I asked some people in uniform passing by; they all said "Eighteen!" and hurried on. I stopped one of them and asked what that was: the 18th floor? Room 18? He laughed, realizing that I was a first-time flier, pointed me to gate number 18 and wished me luck.

My brother Lyonya met me at the John F. Kennedy airport in New York. I hadn't seen him in 12 years, either. He was different: a black kippah on his head; a greying beard; a stooping posture that made him seem shorter; halting speech. He took my bag and drove me in his car to his home, to Brooklyn. Strange streets rolled past the car window.

On the way, Lyonya told me about Mother's illness and said that his wife Ruth would take me there right away.

What, at 8 pm? Who was going to let me in this late in the day? But Lyonya assured me that it would be OK.

We drove up to Lyonya's house in the Borough Park neighborhood of Brooklyn. A small, two-story brick building in a row of similar houses. His wife Ruth, a tall, handsome woman in a long dress and a kerchief, met us, embraced me, welcoming me in English and Russian. This was my first time meeting her, meeting their small children — five boys and a seven-months-old girl. The phone rang while we were exchanging greetings; Lyonya answered, mixing Russian and English words, and said that that was Mother and she was expecting me. Ruth put on her coat to walk me there: it was a ten-minute walk from their house to the hospital. It was cold and dark outside, a January night. At the hospital, no one stopped us, no one demanded that we surrender our winter coats and hats; we walked freely toward the elevators and into Mother's room.

The woman who had left me 12 years before had been beautiful, full of energy, and a little over sixty. The woman in the hospital bed was small, old, gray-haired. Only the eyes were the same: large, dark-brown, shining with love — Mother's eyes. We all cried...

It seemed that half the hospital staff came over to greet the daughter from the Soviet Union. I tried to muster up my poor English to answer their questions, cringing to hear myself make mistakes, but everyone was amazingly friendly and seemed to understand me regardless of my mistakes. Mother was drinking me in with her eyes.

Ruth gave me some time with Mother and then said we should go and could come back the next day. Mother agreed; I could see that all the excitement had made her tired.

We went out of the hospital and walked home in the dark. I looked up and was amazed to see the same Big Dipper as back home, half the world away, except here it was turned sideways.

We came home and had a bite to eat. Lyonya said a Hebrew blessing before the meal: that was new to me. Then Ruth took me up to the little apartment on the second floor where Mother lived and where I would stay while Mother was in the hospital. I was tired out by jet lag, by all the emotions, but nevertheless slept poorly the first night from overstimulation, hearing strange sounds coming through the window; even the air smelled different than in Moscow.

Mother had told me, in her infrequent letters and phone calls, that Lyonya had become a religious Jew, and his family followed strict religious observance in its daily life. Now I saw and experienced it myself. They didn't eat meat and dairy together, didn't speak on the phone or drive a car on Shabbat (Friday night to Sunday morning), and much else besides. It took some getting used to.

The next day it snowed, the streets and trees were all white just like in Moscow—Lyonya said they hadn't had so much snow in years. Ruth and I walked to the hospital, lifting our feet high to step over the snowdrifts. When we arrived, the hospital cook brought in a big cake with pink, blue-bordered icing, with white lettering on it that said: "Welcome to America!" I cried...

The doctor came in. I understood him better than I could speak myself, but I did ask whether it was possible to slow down the disease and extend Mother's life. He gave an honest but devastating answer: no hope.

I brought the cake home but Lyonya threw it out immediately, not letting anyone taste it, because it wasn't kosher.

107

* * *

I went to visit Mother every day. For me, fresh out of the Soviet Union, her hospital was one of the wonders of the world. I had spent enough time in Soviet hospitals, delivering Masha and having a couple of surgeries, so I had a basis for comparison. Where everything in Soviet hospitals seemed calculated to humiliate and oppress the patient, everything in this American hospital seemed to be designed with a view to maximum respect, comfort and reassurance. Mother shared a room with one other person; I had shared with thirty-nine other people. The doctor, when he came to examine her, closed the curtain that was hanging from the ceiling to protect her privacy. It is telling that there is no word for "privacy" in the Russian language because there was no concept of privacy at all in Soviet life. Soviet doctors pulled back the covers in full view of everyone, discussed even the most intimate things in a loud voice and might even raise their voice at a patient who was slow to sit up or turn over as instructed. The country that elevated the collective over the individual was a country of little tyrants: everyone, from the lowliest cleaning lady to the nurse to the doctor, treated patients not as customers to be served but as subjects to be oppressed and bossed around at every turn, if not downright interlopers interrupting their important business. Interestingly, the meanest and nastiest Soviet doctors were women obstetricians and gynecologists, especially at maternity hospitals. I could never understand why...

Mother's room had its own bathroom with a shower, with a door that locked from the inside. Fresh-smelling, with spotless white tiles and a pull cord by the shower stall that summoned a nurse in case of emergency. My Soviet hospital had one bathroom for the whole floor that was locked from the outside; patients were allowed one shower a week; the walls and the tub were too repulsive to touch.

I was also amazed at the hospital cafeteria, at the fact that the staff knew each patient's dietary restrictions and the meals were delivered on a little rolling cart, with a glass of juice and a plate of fresh fruit for everyone for break-fast — an unheard-of luxury in the USSR. It was as though I had stepped through the looking glass!

Lyonya told me that Mother had been ill for a while but hadn't wanted to upset me and therefore had never talked about it in her letters. She had taken a turn for the worse a month ago, right around the time I woke up in the middle of the night.

* * *

He also told me about his religion. He was an ultra-Orthodox Jew, a Hassid, a follower of the fundamentalist Sathmar movement named after its founder, a Hungarian rabbi. There were also other movements within Hasidism, the main one being the Lubavitchers, who were however less restrictive than the Sathmars.

I tried to follow all the house rules about kashrut and Shabbat, but there was so much I didn't know. For example, I didn't know that women were not supposed to look men in the eye and shake their hands, especially not rabbis, and tried to do both when Lyonya's rabbi came to visit. Ruth tutored me in the nuances of acceptable conduct.

I had no such issues with the boys, especially the youngest, who was not yet three years old and therefore had long hair, like a girl, according to Jewish custom. I often played with them all on the floor, to much mutual delight.

Evenings I spent in the basement, half of which was taken up by bookshelves with books from Lyonya's prior life, including a lot of Soviet dissident literature, both *samizdat* and *tamizdat*. There I read *The Oak and the Calf*, a memoir by Solzhenitsyn that talked about his inability to get his work published in the Soviet Union and about his expulsion from the country: he was brought to the airport under armed escort and placed on a plane and was never even told where his flight was headed.

❖ ❖ ❖

After the first week I began to leave the house on weekends to go see some friends and other relatives. I met Mother's younger brother Lou and his wife Sylvia and spent a weekend with them. Their two sons with their wives came over to meet me. Uncle Lou turned out to be very argumentative and enamored of socialism. This surprised me: I had assumed that everyone out in the "real world," especially in America, had long realized how terrible socialism was. Even Uncle Lou's own life, though he refused to admit it, was a testimony in favor of capitalism. He didn't go to college after high school but became an electrician instead, before deciding, several years later, to go back to school and get a college degree. He paid for his education with a bank loan and paid the loan back later with his earnings. A successful life, determined by his own choices and hard work. My father had told me once that American millionaires liked to boast about starting out as dishwashers or waiters or car wash attendants before they established their own businesses and went on to make their millions. I felt uncomfortable arguing with Uncle Lou, preferring to preserve peace and a good relationship with my newfound family.

* * *

A few days after my arrival I got a call from my childhood friend Misha Brin. He had left the Soviet Union several years ago with his wife and their six-year-old son Sergey (the future founder of Google). Now they had another son, a baby, born here in America. Misha started asking how I had made it past the Iron Curtain, and how I got past the government restrictions, and other incredibly sensitive things that one never discussed on the telephone back home. I began to hem and haw, and Misha, understanding my concern, told me to stop it: "You're not in the Soviet Union, you're in America, here you can talk freely on the phone!"

I gave him a brief summary, he invited me to come see them at their house in College Park, Maryland, and one Friday Lyonya gave me money for the ticket and I went. The train ride took three hours. The past several weeks of living at Lyonya's and speaking with Mother's nurses and doctors had restored my confidence: my childhood English was slowly coming back. I ordered lunch in the dining car and had a conversation with a fellow passenger in my train compartment, watching transfixed as she ate an impossibly tall sandwich filled with meat and lettuce without letting a single shred of it fall out. I should learn to eat like that, I thought.

Misha told me about his family's journey—they had left the Soviet Union a few years earlier. Now he was teaching math at the University of Maryland. His wife Zhenya worked for a Government agency, and his mother, Maya, was teaching Russian at the University of Maryland. I was delighted to see them all; we had so much to talk about.

Misha and Zhenya took me around and showed me the sights. Zhenya took me shopping and bought some nice

With Zhenya, Maya and Michael Brin with his dog Bosya
College Park, MD, 1983

clothes for me and Masha. What excited me most were sta-
tionery stores—especially such simple things as "white-
out," the correction fluid that would have saved Volodya
and me so much cutting and pasting! I was also struck by
the ubiquity of restaurants and eateries, which were everywhere: did Americans really need so many places to eat—
when did they have time to do their other business?

❋ ❋ ❋

Misha said that my relative, Bernard Tenenbaum, wanted to see me. Bernard had read about Lyonya in a newspaper—about Lyonya's struggle to have the Soviets recognize
his U.S. citizenship, about his arrest and the week he spent
in jail in Moscow.

In fact, Bernard knew more about all that than I did. Mother and Lyonya had told me nothing when I was pregnant and then nursing my newborn Masha. Only now did Lyonya begin to tell me about his civil rights work and his political activism on behalf of the Jews trying to emigrate from the Soviet Union. He told me about the Moscow Synagogue where young Jews used to gather on Jewish holidays and dance in a circle under the eye of the police, who stood on the sidewalk but didn't bother them. One year on Yom Kippur, two visiting Brooklyn rabbis, Rabbi Greer and Rabbi Frick, went there hoping to meet Soviet Jews and were surprised when Lyonya addressed them in English. He invited them home, promising them a chance to speak with his mother and hear her genuine Brooklyn accent. They came and heard her tell her story, and Lyonya talked about the plight of the Soviet dissidents and minorities, especially the Jews. That's when the rabbis mentioned that, under U.S. law, both Mother and Lyonya remained U.S. citizens. Rabbi Greer was a lawyer by training and knew what needed to be done to confirm Lyonya's U.S. citizenship and get U.S. passports for both of them. This was eventually done.

I had had it in the back of my head to go to the U. S. State Department and ask for their help in getting us out of the Soviet Union. Now Lyonya told me I had the same right to U.S. citizenship as he did, and Misha made an appointment for me at the State Department and also set a date for me to meet with Bernard Tenenbaum.

When we first spoke on the phone, Bernard said he would be wearing a blue suit. Here, my still-wobbly English let me down slightly: my Russian textbooks had translated the English word "blue" as sky-blue or baby-blue, making me wonder at these American fashions, since Russians did not wear light-colored clothes in winter. I stood on the steps of the State Department building, an outlandish sight in my old Russian shearling coat and fur hat; the day was cold but there was no snow, and most people went around with their heads uncovered. A small red car pulled up, and a tall, energetic, pleasant-looking man in a dark navy business suit got out. We started talking; Bernard had lots of questions, and so did I. In my excitement, I forgot much of my English, especially all the verb tenses, but somehow we understood each other. I poured out a jumble of words, and Bernard formed them into sentences and spoke them back to me. In this way, we had a conversation.

Bernard took me to lunch at the Watergate Hotel, of Richard Nixon's notoriety, and ordered a steak for me. We spent a long time talking, and then he took me to his home, where I met his wife Ellen and his two little girls: eighteen-months-old Karen, bravely toddling around, and baby Emily, whom I happily held and fed from a bottle. Their home was warm and welcoming, and I enjoyed my time with them despite my language problems; besides, Bernard was family, an actual blood cousin—what joy!

During a subsequent visit, Bernard introduced me to another cousin, Amity Horowitz, who lived in Virginia with her husband Danny and two sons. Her oldest, Jesse, enthusiastically played horsie with his younger brother Eli and Bernard's daughter Karen, carrying them on his back. I reveled in my newfound family, making up for a lifetime of loneliness back in the Soviet Union.

We talked a lot. I told them about our life, about the difficulties of being Jewish in the Soviet Union, especially with an American mother. I felt that they understood me.

Bernard asked me what we thought we would do once we got to the U.S. I said that Volodya was prepared to do any work at all, even work at a McDonald's, and so was I, so I was sure we would find some kind of work. We were mentally prepared for the move to America and were reading a lot and studying English, and had found an English teacher for Masha as well.

Bernard and Amity were my cousins on my father's side. Uncle Lou was my mother's brother, and I also met another cousin on that side, Gerri Gelber, the daughter of Mother's sister, who lived on Long Island with her husband Peter and their children in a house overlooking Long Island Sound. Gerri and Peter showed me around New York. One day, Gerri took me to lunch and left the tip right out in the open, on the table. I commented that anyone might see the money and pocket it. "They won't," she said. "How can you be sure?" "Everyone knows this money is for the waiter. Everyone leaves tips on the table, and no one steals it." Such were the people the Soviet media had branded as greedy capitalists, devoid of conscience and compassion.

* * *

Although I tried to stay away from politics, I was constantly surprised to find that my American family saw these issues very differently. To me, there was a direct progression from the views that were called "liberal" in the American political landscape to socialism; and hadn't Vladimir Lenin himself said that the goal of socialism was communism? But wasn't American prosperity the result of free enterprise and respect for private property that was the cornerstone of capitalism? And hadn't Socialist regimes caused squalor and human misery in every country where they had been built, including the one I had come from?

I had, and still have, a deep-seated moral objection to all forms of coercive redistribution of wealth and attempts to equalize social and economic outcomes. Since then, I've had an opportunity to observe that the loudest calls for redistribution tend to come from people who are themselves economically secure, if not prosperous, like the leadership of the Democratic party, and who never seem to volunteer to give their own wealth away. I have the deepest affection and gratitude for this country and its people and hope that they do not repeat the errors made by so many other countries.

* * *

My visa was about to expire, and Lyonya said we should mail my Soviet passport to the State Department to have the visa extended. He placed the passport in an envelope together with a check and started to seal it. "Are you really going to send it by regular mail?" I asked, aghast. "What if it gets lost in the mail—what will I do without a passport?" Lyonya and Ruth laughed: this was America, it would be OK. And it was: ten days later, my passport came back in the mail, stamped with my new visa.

Eventually, Mother was discharged from the hospital. Due to a scheduling mix-up, they brought her home at a time when no one was home because Ruth had taken me to a kosher bakery to get some cookies. We returned to find Mother sitting in her wheelchair in front of the house. I was surprised that they had left her all alone; that wasn't right. But I had never seen such wheelchairs before: the chair was a marvel of engineering and comfort, another sign of respect and care for the individual.

* * *

Mother moved back into her apartment, and I moved onto a cot in the living room. One Friday night, Uncle Lou came in his car to take me away for the weekend. Mother became worried, nervously telling him to go quickly, before Lyonya saw this desecration of Shabbat. The next morning — on Saturday — Lyonya called Uncle Lou's house and said that Mother had passed away and I should come back right away. In this way, I learned that Orthodox Judaism permits certain things on Shabbat in the event of death, like speaking on the phone and driving cars. I was glad I had said goodbye to Mother; I kept feeling her lips on my cheek and her arms around me.

Now I had a chance to observe the Jewish funeral customs. Ruth translated some of the synagogue service for me from Hebrew, but I found that I was able to feel the emotion of it even without knowing the words. I suspect that all daughters feel the same things after losing their mothers, regardless of language or geography.

* * *

It soon emerged that Mother's death had greatly complicated my plans to leave the Soviet Union with Volodya and Masha. The American side required an "affidavit of relationship" from my American relatives, as well as another document, Affidavit of Support, showing their willingness to provide financial support for me and my family if we were admitted into the country. My brother Lyonya, my next of kin, signed the former but was advised by his rabbi not to sign the latter. He had six children to feed on one income and was afraid that we might become a burden to his family. Indeed, he probably thought, what work could a teacher of Russian and a translator from Russian into French hope to find in America?

Lyonya told me that Mother had left no will and that he had spent so much on her hospital bills that he couldn't give me any of the money she had left. I didn't argue, although it added to the pain. Ruth heard this conversation and said nothing but went upstairs and brought down a few of Mother's metal figurines and gave them to me as a memento; something of Mother's, at least.

On the other hand, I was grateful to Lyonya for all the financial support he provided while I stayed with him. He paid for my weekend trips to Maryland and Baltimore to visit Misha, Bernard and others. He also paid what I felt was an exorbitant amount for my new glasses. And he paid for my plane ticket home.

Though I didn't know it at the time, my dear cousin Bernard spoke with Maya and Misha after I left, and together they went into action. As a result of their efforts, a Jewish organization named HIAS (The Hebrew Immigrant Aid Society) that helped resettle political refugees in the U.S. agreed to take our case. Although our case was a complicated one—I was a U.S. citizen but Volodya and Masha weren't—they were able to secure certain government benefits for us, including direct financial assistance and, most importantly, medical insurance, which had been Lyonya's main concern given the high cost of medical care in the U.S.

All this, however, was four years into the future, and in the meantime, I had a plane to catch back to Moscow. Uncle Lou drove me to the airport. I think I shocked him a little: when he asked what had impressed me the most about America, I said: "Public restrooms." I told him that to me, clean public restrooms were a sign of a prevailing culture of dignity, self-respect and respect for others that was so glaringly absent back home.

* * *

Volodya and Masha met me at the airport — my dearest ones whom I had missed so much and was so happy to see again.

Volodya grilled me all night, asking questions, wanting to know the smallest details. The next day I had a terrible headache, probably from jet lag. We were out of headache medicine, and I went to the pharmacy. I paid for the medicine at the cashier's window, walked over to the dispensing counter and handed my receipt to the clerk. She tossed the box of pills on the counter and turned away to resume her chat with another clerk. I stood there, waiting — expecting her to put the medicine in a plastic bag, to smile and to thank me for my purchase. The two clerks looked back at me, perplexed: what was my problem? I smiled bitterly and left. Buck up, my dear, I said to myself, you're not in America anymore; you're back in the USSR where no one wraps your purchases, and no one smiles, and no one says thank you. I was only gone for three months but I had gotten used to being treated like a human being. It was going to be tough to unlearn.

The same Boris Lempert took me to Spaso House, the official residence of the U.S. ambassador in Moscow where the ambassador, Arthur Hartman, gave parties, organized screenings of American movies, meetings with interesting people, etc. Boris introduced me to embassy staff and to five other people who, like me, held dual Soviet and American citizenship. The embassy people took an interest in us and began inviting us to various events. Once we met with Elie Wiesel, a writer and Holocaust survivor, former prisoner of the Nazi death camps of Auschwitz and Buchenwald. Another time they got us two tickets to a concert of the famous jazz musician David Brubeck who was visiting Moscow. Volodya could not come because he was not allowed any contacts with foreigners due to his work. We were under surveillance, and a contact with Americans might cost him his job, if not an arrest on some sort of espionage charge. I took Masha with me instead. Unfortunately, she was having an awkward "teenage moment" and refused to say anything good about the wonderful music. Ironically, now, as an adult, she loves jazz.

* * *

In 1985, Mikhail Gorbachev came to power, ushering in a new era of *perestroika* (restructuring) and *glasnost* (openness) and generally trying to put a human face on the regime. We were having lunch in the kitchen, the TV was rumbling on in the living room, when a speech by Gorbachev was announced—and we heard something one never, ever heard on TV: the sound of ordinary, unscripted human speech. Government officials always spoke in stilted, formal, droning tones, so to hear the head of the country speak as though he had just stopped by for a chat was sensational. We ran to the living room and gaped at the TV, all thoughts of lunch forgotten. Of course, Gorbachev was attempting the impossible: the regime could not be both humane and communist, and eventually even the partial reforms he had unleashed (coupled with the economically crippling arms race and the Cold war the the Soviets claimed started by Ronald Reagan) would bring it down.

* * *

April 1987. The then U. S. Secretary of State George Shultz came to Moscow for talks with Gorbachev. On April 14, the U.S. embassy held a Passover Seder at Spaso House for Soviet Jewish *refuseniks*. Among the guests were my new dual-citizen friends and Abigail Scharansky, the wife of Natan Scharansky.

George Shultz, although not Jewish himself, attended the Seder wearing a kippah as a sign of respect. He went up to each of us, introduced himself, asked our names and shook our hands.

These were the late 1980s; U.S.-Soviet relations were in flux, and it was known that at each official high-level meeting, the Americans presented a list of names of Jewish families whose release they were requesting. Our *refusenik* friends who had just received their permissoins to emigrate joked that now was my turn, and I would be presented to George Shultz as a gift, as it were, with a big bow on top, as part of the latest negotiations. Apparently, that is indeed what happened, because the next day, on April 15, the phone rang, and an official-sounding female voice asked for me, using my full legal name (with the patronymic). Then there was a bit of mumbling on the line, from which it emerged that if we were to file again, our application to emigrate might be approved.

After that, we had to submit mountains of documents with our application, including an affidavit from Volodya's parents stating that he had no outstanding financial obligations to them and they had no objection to his leaving. We were allowed to exchange Soviet rubles to receive 420 dollars for the three of us, 200 of those were in the form of travelers checks which we didn't even know how to use. We were also told to produce a paper from Masha's school, since our case was being processed prior to Masha's final exams at school; this could have made her life there miserable in the remaining months of the school year. "Nope, not doing that," I said calmly, looking the visa official in the eye. "Whaaaat?" The poor woman, unused to being contradicted and unsure how to react to such effrontery, turned pale, then beet-red. I said: "I don't know if you people will actually let us out or not, and I'm not going to ruin my daughter's life over this." The woman, at a loss for words, finally accepted our documents. I never knew that standing up to Soviet bureaucracy would feel so good!

On the American side, my cousin Bernard, working with Misha and the helpful people at the State Department, put together all the necessary documents proving my U.S. citizenship, and soon I stood before the U. S. Consul in Moscow to receive my U.S. passport and take an oath, swearing that all the information I had submitted was true, that I would not engage or participate in subversive activity, and that I would respect and protect the laws and the Constitution of the United States of America. I will never forget the solemnity of the moment.

It didn't happen without a hiccup on the Soviet side. Since U. S. Embassies abroad are considered to be part of U.S. territory and not that of the host country, they are guarded not only by U.S. forces but also by host country forces, since to enter one is to cross the border. The Soviet police guarding the approaches to the embassy stopped me and took me to a little booth to the side of the entrance, where they took my Soviet passport and left me alone. Thankfully, at such critical moments, women can always pull out a mirror and powder their nose, fix their hair, etc.: anything to help pass the time while not showing any fear or nervousness. Finally, I heard voices in the back, and soon after that they handed me back my passport and took me to the consular department.

Finally, all the formalities were complete, and on June 9, 1987 we left the country. As always, the Soviet regime had one last insult in store for us. We were taking a small china tea set in one of our suitcases, all carefully packed with paper, but the customs man opened every bag, pawed through each item, and then slammed the covers back down and pressed down with the heel of his hand, with a nasty smirk on his face. The tea set arrived in the U.S. in tiny little china shards: only one cup and one plate remained intact. We called this our "inoculation against nostalgia".

There was also a hold-up at passport control. I was traveling on my Soviet passport, with my U.S. passport packed in our luggage. Volodya's and Masha's Soviet passports, stamped with U.S. entry visas, were returned without comment, but my passport had no visa, since I was going to enter the U.S. as a citizen, using my U.S. passport. The young clerk was so frightened by this irregularity that a sheen of sweat came out on his forehead. He conferred with a colleague standing nearby, then got on the phone. We were getting really worried: our Pan Am flight was due to take off in a matter of minutes. A flight attendant ran over to tell us that they were holding the flight and wouldn't leave without us. At last, a KGB man came out and waved us through.

While all this was going on, all the business class seats on the plane filled up, so we ended up in the first class section. After we were finally airborne, Volodya touched my hand and said, in a conspiratorial whisper: "We're carrying contraband!" My heart sank. Then he touched my hand again, and, grinning from ear to ear, pointed to Masha: "We're smuggling her out! We're stealing her away from them!"

He was right. And it was wonderful. We've felt it keenly through all our years here, and Volodya thought about it until his last day.

In New York, we got off the plane and followed the crowd to a sign that directed U.S. citizens to the right and non-citizens to the left. But our family included both: where should we go? Well, I thought, since I got us into this, it's on me to figure it out. I gathered up all my English and, surprised at my own boldness, marched up to a tall man who was standing by the sign and directing the flow of arriving passengers with a stream of joking banter. "Sir," I said, craning my neck to look up at him, "our family has both citizens and non-citizens: what should we do?" The man paused for a second, looking at me, then smiled broadly and said: "I know who you are: you're Janet Kotler!" That's when I knew that all our troubles were behind us. The man was a HIAS official named Gerry; he was there specifically to meet our family. Later, I would work with him at HIAS.

Thus began —

LIFE: PART TWO

Gerry took us to a little hotel in Manhattan, where we were given a small room with two beds. As we later realized, the hotel, though located in the back streets off 6th Avenue, was not luxurious at all; in fact, it was something of a roach motel. Even so, the room was equipped with a working air conditioner; the bathroom had functioning hot- and cold-water faucets and a big stack of clean towels on a shelf over the commode. The room was supplied with coffee but no tea, and since Masha was not (and is not) a coffee drinker, we asked Volodya to go down to a little shop across the street. He was gone so long that I began to worry and came back pale, empty-handed and irritated: "They had so much tea—this kind and that kind and the other kind—I didn't know which to buy!"* I went down a little later and bought some tea, and eventually we found our way and learned to navigate our new life.

The next day, Bernard came to take us for a river cruise around Manhattan. He asked about our flight, our accommodations. During the cruise he pointed out the sights, all the while talking to Volodya about job interviews and how to prepare for them, and what a resume was and how to write one. I mentioned that the Soviet

---

* He was not alone in this. In the 1984 film *Moscow on the Hudson*, actor Robin Williams plays a Russian defector who faints in the coffee aisle when confronted with the abundant choices. It is a physical feeling, not unlike a punch to the stomach, causing dizziness and light-headedness.

customs people had taken away our sewing supplies (needles, thread, etc.), so after the cruise Bernard took us to a 7-11, which impressed me greatly and where I bought what I needed.

Then Ruth and Lyonya invited us over. They had rented a furnished apartment for us down the street from their house in the Jewish neighborhood of Borough Park in Brooklyn. Their congregation had donated 28 whole frozen chickens for us. Since they wouldn't all fit in our freezer, Ruth gave them to me in batches over time. We were endlessly grateful to all these people for their generosity, and I had to stretch my culinary skills to their limit to find new ways of cooking chicken.

We also went to visit Volodya's uncle Lyova who had come to the U.S. from Kiev in the Ukraine a few years earlier. He lived with his family in the Brighton Beach neighborhood of Brooklyn. Their neighbours and friends donated some dishes and other household things for us.

We marveled at the kindness and courtesy of total strangers. People smiled at us in the street. On a subway ride from Brooklyn to Manhattan, in a car where the air conditioner wasn't working, Masha was overcome by the heat. Passengers around us jumped up to give us their seats, someone offered us a bottle of water, someone else gave us a cool, damp handkerchief to put on her forehead.

As I said in the beginning, it has been over three decades since we came to America. We are still grateful for everything: for the smiles of strangers; for that police car that stopped and waved me through at an intersection; for the care and patience of medical staff, from specialist doctors to nurses to janitors; for the drivers who

Author with her daughter Masha
Arlington, Virginia

stop their cars to let me cross and catch my bus on the other side of the street. And most of all, I am grateful to my wonderful relatives: Bernard and Ellen Tenenbaum, Amity and Danny Horowitz, Gerri and Peter Gelber, and many others who made us feel welcome in America.

We love you forever.

FAMILY OF HENRY RIGERMAN

Aryeh Leib Rigerman, brother of Ada Rigerman-Ashmon, came to America in 1907 from a *shtetl* of Kublichi in what is now Belarus, leaving behind his wife Gittel and young son Henry (Hendel). They came to join him in Boston five years later. Gittel eventually returned to Kublichi with Henry. Aryeh married Rose Jacobson in 1915; they had no children. Aryeh ran various businesses, from selling fruit and candy to running a lodging-house. In 1924, Aryeh became an American citizen, changing his name to Louis Rigerman. He died in 1935.

His son Henry returned to America in 1925 to live with his father; the whole *shtetl* had donated money to fund his trip. In 1931, Henry married Esther Michael, daughter of a local tailor.

The same year, influenced, no doubt, by the turmoil of the Great Depression (which sparked an increase in anti-Semitism), and perhaps by some Communist friends, the newlyweds emigrated to the Soviet Union. They settled in Moscow, where they shared a Government-assigned three room *communal apartment* with another family. The two families shared the kitchen and the bathroom and kept their voices low: loose lips could land them in Siberia. Gittel lived with them until her death in 1946.

Henry escaped the purges by leaving his job at the Ministry of Meat and Dairy, where he was working on the American food assistance program known as the Lend Lease. From then on and until his death in 1967, he would fly below the NKVD's radar by working as a freelance translator for scientific research organizations and news agencies. He was more fortunate than many of his fellow idealistic Western expats, who perished in slave labor camps.

Henry and Esther's son, Leonid, was born in 1940. Their daughter Janet (Zhanna) was born in 1944. Between these two dates lay WWII and a flight to Kuybyshev (now Samara), some 1500 miles to the east, away from the advancing Germans.

Leonid Rigerman was active in the nascent human rights movement of the 1960s–1970s, which advocated the right of Russian Jews to leave the Soviet Union, at a time when travel outside the "iron curtain" was severely restricted. In 1970, Leonid waged a very public campaign to have his American citizenship recognized by the authorities — an uphill battle, since his parents had been coerced into renouncing their American citizenship upon arrival and the Soviet Union did not recognize dual citizenship. Leonid spent a week in jail, while his American friends launched an international media campaign to free him; Leonid and Esther's photos appeared in newspapers. Upon his release, in January 1971, Leonid and Esther were allowed to emigrate to the U. S. They live in Brooklyn, NY, surrounded by an abundance of children and grandchildren.

Janet married Volodya (Vladimir) Kotler in 1965 and had a daughter, Masha (Marie), in 1970. In 1979, the Kotlers applied for permission to emigrate to the U. S. Like many others, they became *refuseniks* when their application was denied. It cost Janet her job as a schoolteacher. For the next eight years, Volodya worked as a freelance translator and Janet stayed home and became involved in *refusenik* circles.

In 1983, Leonid sent word that Esther was dying. With great difficulty, Janet obtained permission to leave the country to visit their mother in the U.S. and was able to be with Esther when she passed in February 1983. That was when Janet first met her American cousins, including Bernard Tenenbaum and Amity Horowitz. The long-lost cousins became great friends. Over the next several years the American branch worked hard to help the Russian branch emigrate and start their new life here; their generosity will never be forgotten.

The Kotlers came to the U.S. in 1987, starting out in Brooklyn, NY and later moving to the Washington, DC area. Their daughter, Masha, lives near them with her husband, Dewey Cochran, and their three children: Jacob, Sara and Danny.

Made in the USA
Monee, IL
04 January 2021